THE STREETS OF
BRUM

PART ONE

2003

THE STREETS OF
BRUM
PART ONE

Carl Chinn

BREWIN BOOKS

First published in 2003 by
Brewin Books, Studley, Warwickshire B80 7LG

British Library Cataloguing in Publication Data
A catalogue record for this book is available from
The British Library

ISBN: 1 858858 245 8

Typeset in Times and made and printed
in Great Britain by Warwick Printing Company Limited,
Caswell Road, Leamington Spa CV31 1QD

To our children and our children's children so that they might understand a little about the city in which they live.

Preface

I have been researching the street names of Birmingham for a number of years. Originally, I had intended that this research would be included in a book that also examined the place names of the city. However, I soon realised that there was much too much information for one book on both subjects and so included material on place names in *1,000 Years of Brum* (Birmingham: Birmingham Evening Mail, 1999). Since this work came out, I have continued to delve into the origins of our street names and now realise that it would be impossible to encompass all that I have found within a single publication. Hence the *Street names of Brum. Part One.*

In this book I have focussed on a variety of streets the names of which begin with the letters A to E. However, within each of the headlined streets there are often discussions of closely related streets that may begin with a letter other than A to E. For example, the section on Colmore Row also includes explanations of Great Charles Street, Margaret Street and Newhall Street – all of which can only be understood in connection with Colmore Row. Such streets are made bold in the text. The headline streets and those made bold are included in the index; whilst where it is necessary, I also draw attention to other headline streets that are of relevance to a particular entry. Some of these headline streets will be in later parts of this work. I expect Part 2 to be out next year and other parts to follow as and when necessary. Because of the style of the book there is no list of contents, although the headline streets are gathered in chapters according to the letter of the alphabet to which they pertain. I hope that you find reading this book as fascinating as I have found its research.

Foreword

Birmingham's streets, roads and lanes are an absorbing yet neglected aspect of our city's history. They call out to us about long dead landowners, notable figures from the history of England, Brummies long forgotten, farms that have been swept away by the outpouring of our city, remarkable physical features, distant battles, intriguing foreign places and mysterious happenings. Such names almost demand of us that we ask questions of them. Why is Conybere Street so called? Where is the Fashoda that is highlighted in a Ten Acres road? How did AB Row gain its name? For what reason are the Adderleys brought to mind in Saltley? Did people wash themselves in Bath Row? And were cherries picked in Cherry Street?

The streets of Brum are a dynamic thing. Like Edgbaston Street, a select handful have been with us since our beginnings as a major town in the later Middle Ages, but hundreds upon hundreds of new streets have appeared with the expansion of the town – and many have disappeared with Birmingham's various redevelopments. Some of these lost streets are expressive and intriguing in their names and lead us to fanciful thoughts about their origins. Why was **Fish Lane**, off Harborne Road, so called and why was it changed to **Bullock Road**? And who decided that Bullock Road was not an attractive name and dropped it in favour of **Kingscote Road** in 1880? How did a **Fisherman's Hut Lane** arise in Nechells, later becoming part of **Aston Church Road**? What were the origins of **Moses Lane**, Yardley and why did it become **Croft Road** in 1927? For what reason was the colourful **Noah's Ark Passage**, off Montague Street, Bordesley, abandoned in 1894 in favour of **Fawdry Street**? And who named the frightening **Devil's Tooth Hollow Yard** and the jump-like **Froggery** – both of which were swept away in the nineteenth century?

Important as are so many of our street names, unfortunately large numbers of them in the modern city are intruders and do not relate to the city, its history, its peoples or its landscape. They have arisen from the whim of builders and others who have imposed names from spots unconnected with Birmingham and its past. This trend became most noticeable in the massive growth of the city from the 1920s, when thousands of acres of farmland were overwhelmed by housing. In Kingstanding, the London builder of the district's corporation homes brought in places from the south east of England, for example in **Colindale Road** and **Charlton Road**. Nearby in Perry Common, another council estate was laid out with roads reaching out to Derbyshire as in **Dovedale Road**, and Sussex, as in **Hastings Road**. Similarly in Bournbrook a number of roads, such as **Tiverton Roa**d, call out to the south west; in Birchfield, the developers favoured names from Kent, of the ilk of **Canterbury Road**, and the west country, like **Tewkesbury Road**; whilst more Derbyshire place names occur in Hall Green, amongst them **Burnaston Road, Cubley Road, Etwall Road** and **Smirrels Road**.

Despite this marked and regretable tendency in the twentieth century towards the use of names unassociated with Birmingham and its history, there remains a fascinating array of indeginous names that we all should look at and learn from. How many of us have walked along a street and wondered whence it hailed? And how important is it for our children and our children's children that they gain a sense of place and stability, a feeling of belonging that surely leads on from an awareness of the place names and street names which embrace their lives? Perhaps one of the biggest problems we are faced with today is an alienated and apparently rootless youth. Hopefully through an understanding of local history, young people can be handed a consciousness of the past that leads them both to gain a sense of self worth and to give respect to others who may be different to them.

Birmingham is not a rootless place, as its street names shout out. Its origins stretch back to 1166 when its lord, Peter of Bermingham, gained a charter entitling him to hold a market. Within a few years the first streets would have emerged, but the earliest documentary evidence naming a street relates to a lane that was outside the borough, that is the built up part of Birmingham gathered around Saint Martin's. This was a release of property in 1289 from Ranulph son of Walter of Barre to Roger of Somerlone – **Summer Lane**. The first street recorded in the emerging town of Birmingham is Edgbastone Strete (**Edgbaston Street**) mentioned in a deed in 1347; and in 1449 Roger Cutte of Erdington granted to John and Juliane Knocks of Birmingham a burgage and butcher's shop in the same street. Another deed from 1437 concerns property in 'Mowlestrete' – **Moor Street**; whilst in 1454, Sir William Bermyngham, the lord of the manor, granted to John of Birmingham one croft of land in **Dale End**. Later in the fifteenth century, in 1482-3, a deed stated that John Lench of **Deritend**, master of the Guild of Holy Cross, with the unanimous assent of the brothers and sisters of the guild, leased to William Wyot a tanner of Birmingham a parcel of land 'lying jux le cawsy' – next to the causeway (see Digbeth).

The detailed researches of Toulmin Smith in the nineteenth century shed light on the origins of a number of streets. He examined a grant of properties to John Pretty from Edward Bermingham, the last of his family to be lord of Birmingham, and dated 1532. These holdings included a water mill to grind corn called Heth Mill, hence **Heath Mill Lane**; lands called the Conyngry, leading to **Congreve Street**; and the Dodwalls, which gave rise to **Dudley Street**. Toulmin Smith's investigation of the 1547 tenants and tenancies of the Guild of the Holy Cross (put down the previous year by Henry VIII) indicates the **Bull Ring;** Chappell Street (see **Bull Street**); Deryatend (see **Deritend High Street**); Dalend (see **Dale End**); Egebaston Street (see **Edgbaston Street**); Englishe Street (see **High Street**); Godes Cart Lane (see **Carrs Lane**); **High Street**; Mercer Street (see **Spiceal Street**); le Pinfolde (**Pinfold Street**); Molle Strete Barres and Molle Strete End (see **Moor Street**); Newe Street (see **New Street**); Parke Strete (see **Park Street**); and **Well Street** (see **Digbeth**).

Six years later, the *Survey of the Borough of Birmingham* (1553) also gave a number of Birmingham's streets. Carried out in the first year of Queen Mary's reign, it followed on from the attainder (forfeiture of land because of treason) of John Dudley, the Duke of Northumberland, who had held Birmingham. This survey indicated a number of others streets: Bordesley (see **Bordesley High Street**); Dudwall Lane (see **Dudley Street**); Dygbeth (see **Digbeth**); Priors Conyngre Lane (see **Congreve Street**); **The Shambles**; **Swan Alley**; and Welch Market (see **High Street**). It can be seen clearly from this list that Birmingham was based on one long street, running from Bordesley High Street along Deritend High Street and Digbeth and into High Street. All the other streets came off this main stretch, and an examination of deeds and tenancies would indicate that Edgbaston Street was the most important of these. This street pattern was shaped like a crescent, leading to some people describing Birmingham as the town of the half moon.

By the time of Bradford's **Plan of Birmingham** of 1750, the earliest map to show street lines and mark the town's boundaries, this street pattern remained obvious – although development had now begun to spread up hill and across the ridge on which Saint Philip's is placed. Bradford lists 93 streets and the number of houses and people in each, giving a population 23,688. The making of these streets was declaimed by Hutton:

> The inhabitants of Birmingham may be styled masters of invention; the Arts are obedient to their will. But if Genius displays herself in the shops, she is seldom seen in the streets; though we have a long time practised the art of making streets, we have an art to learn; there is not a street in the whole town but might have been better constructed. When land is appropriated for a street, the builders are under no control; every lessee proceeds according to his interest or fancy; there is no man to preserve order, or prescribe bounds; hence arise evils without a cure; such as a narrowness which scarcely admits light, cleanliness, pleasure, health, or use; unneccesary hills, like that in Bull Street; sudden falls, owing to the floor of one house being laid three feet lower than the next, as in Coleshill Street; one side of a street, like the deck of a ship, 'gunnel to', several feet higher than the other, as in Snow Hill, New Street, Friday Street, Paradise Row, Lionel Street, Suffolk Street, Brick-kiln Lane, and Great Charles Street.

Hutton published his first edition of his *History of Birmingham* in 1780. By this time, the town had begun an extraodinary rise on to the world stage through its manufacturing prowess. As its repuation waxed and its products increased, so too did the number of its people and the streets in which they lived. Birmingham entered upon a period of almost continual change, whereby new streets were cut out of farmland and old ones were swept away in redevelopments. Such transformations led James Dobbs in 1828 to write the song 'I Can't Find Brummagem'.

I Can't Find Brummagem

Full twenty years and more are passed
Since I left Brummagem.
But I set out for home at last
To good old Brummagem.
But ev'ry place is altered so
Now there's hardly a place I know
Which fills my heart with grief and woe
For I can't find Brummagem.

As I was walking down the street
As used to be in Brummagem,
I knowed nobody I did meet
For they've changed their face in Brummagem
Poor old Spiceal Street's half gone,
And Old Church stands alone
And poor old I stands here to groan
For I can't find Brummagem.

But amongst the changes we have got
In good old Brummagem
They've made a market on the moat
To sell the pigs in Brummagem.
But that has brought us more ill luck
For they've filled up Pudding Brook,
Where in the brook jack-bannils took
Near Good old Brummagem.

But what's more melancholy still,
For poor old Brummagem,
They've taken away all Newhall-Hill
From poor old Brummagem,
At Easter time girls fair and brown,
Came roly-poly down,
And showed their legs to half the town,
Oh! the good old sights in Brummagem.

Down Peck Lane I walked along,
To find out Brummagem,
There was the dungil down and gone
What? no rogues in Brummagem,

They've ta'en it to a street called Moor,
A sign that rogues ain't fewer,
But rogues won't like it there I'm sure,
While Peck Lane's in Brummagem.

I remember one John Growse,
Who buckles made in Brummagem,
He built himself a country house,
To be out of the smoke of Brummagem
But though John's country house stands still,
The town has walked up hill,
Now he lives beside a smoky mill,
In the middle of Brummagem.

Among the changes that abound
In good old Brummagem,
May trade and happiness be found
In good old Brummagem.
And tho' no Newhall Hill we've got
Nor Pudding Brook nor Moat,
May we always have enough
To boil the pot in Brummagem.

Dobbs was a comedian and performed this song first at the Theatre Royal, New Street in 1828. Though written humorously, it has at its heart a lament at the loss of well-known streets. It is through this melding of wit and poignancy that Dobbs reaches out to each generation of Brummies. For in each generation, developers and planners seem to take our city, knock it down and replace it with new buildings and places. Brummies ourselves are too often excluded from the process of redevelopment, so that there is a sense of loss in each generation for the streets in which once we lived, shopped and worked and which have been chucked so carelessly into the miskin of history. The streets of Brum and their people deserve better.

Bradford's record of 93 streets focused on the built-up part of Birmingham and does not mention Summer Lane or other routes in the then farmland districts such as Hockley, Brookfields, Winson Green, Spring Hill, Rotton Park and Ladywood. And of course, it excludes all those districts that were not then part of Birmingham, including Aston, Balsall Heath, Erdington, Handsworth, Harborne, Kings Norton, Little Bromwich, Northfield, Ward End and Yardley – and all the areas belonging to them, like Lozells, Short Heath, Handsworth Wood, Moseley, Weoley Castle and Sparkhill. Bearing this in mind, Bradford listed 50 streets, ten lanes, six alleys, four rows, two squares, one court and one green. These were supplemented by a variety of streets known by just a name – as with Corn Cheaping, Deritend, Digbeth, Froggary, High Town (High Street), Lower Minories, Lower Priory and others. Within a generation the number of streets had risen markedly. The *Birmingham Directory* of 1777, one of the first such compilations, gives 148 streets with various endings – the most popular of which was street.

As a word, street derives from the Latin 'strata via', meaning paved way, becoming 'straet' in Old English. The Anglo-Saxons used street in the names of settlements close to a Roman road, as with Stirchley (originally Strutley) and Streetly. Both are close to the **Icknield Street,** which struck through what is now Birmingham and both meant the clearing (ley) by the street. Later, streets emerged within settlements. Usually they were associated with main thoroughfares and often indicated a route to somewhere, for example with **Edgbaston Street**. Generally, the Old English word for road was 'weg', meaning way, as in **Holloway Head**. Victor Skipp has rescued for us two Anglo-Saxon ways in Yardley. The first was **Dagardingweg** on the Sheldon and Yardley border. It can be followed still as a pathway across Kent's Moat Park, before becoming **Pool Way** and then **Broadstone Road**. The second was **Leommannincgweg**, which Skipp feels may be what is now the **Stratford Road**.

The term path was used for unmade roads that went across open country; whilst in modern times, a lane raises up visions of rural settings. However, in earlier periods it was often used for a narrow street in a town, like with **Peck Lane**. As Birmingham expanded, these urban lanes were supplemented by lanes that had been in the country. These were longer and often wider. There are a number of examples, including **Sandy Lane**, **Summer Lane** and **Watery Lane** – the suggestive names of which indicate the nature of the particular route.

As for the term road, it is from the Old English word 'rad', from 'ridan', meaning to ride. This origin may explain the use of the term 'orse road' by working-class Brummies when warning their children 'to mind the 'orse road'. Road occurs only once in Shakespeare and it remained unusual until the eighteenth century when it was used in association with the building of military routes in Scotland and turnpikes in England. Administered by trusts authorised by private acts of Parliament, turnpikes took their name from a pike that formed a barrier to traffic and that was turned to allow access. These turnpike trusts were empowered to levy tolls on travellers. The money raised was spent on the upkeep and maintenance of the route. This involved the digging of drainage ditches and laying down a surface of stones and cinders.

For many years the word road was restricted to these turnpikes that led to other places, such as the **Alcester Road**, **Bristol Road**, **Coventry Road** and **Dudley Road**. Road was also applied to routes that were not turnpikes but which went to a nearby village or town, as with the **Aston Road** and **Saltley Road**. But as late as 1834, *Guest's Plan of Birmingham* included little more than a handful of roads, only four which were not linked with a route to a place outside Birmingham. These were **Asylum Road**, Summer Lane; **Tookey's Road**, Hockley, about which there is no information and which is not indicated elsewhere; and **Lee Bank Road** and **Wellington Road**, Edgbaston. Over the next thirty-odd years, a few more roads appeared, but from the 1870s there was a massive increase in their number. This extraordinary rise was tied up with the issue of class.

The development of the locality of The Square (**Old Square**) in the early eighteenth century allowed manufacturers, merchants and professionals to move away from the lower ground of Digbeth and up the hill to a drier and healthier spot that afforded good views. As Birmingham developed, this area became surrounded by manufactories and was enveloped in pollution and so the middle class moved again, this time south west to the Calthorpe Estate in Edgbaston, and north west to Handsworth. Lying in the direction of the prevailing winds in England, Edgbaston was particularly attractive because it was upwind of the smoke and smells of Birmingham. It had the added advantage of falling mostly within the ownership of one family under whose direction the area was developed as a middle-class enclave. With the flight of the more prosperous and the pouring in of migrants from the villages around Birmingham, the large dwellings of the wealthy were turned into lodging houses, as in Park Street, whilst the gardens and open spaces in Digbeth and in and around Old Square were filled in with workshops and back-to-back houses. This infilling increased the overcrowding and industrial fumes and so led to the connection of streets with the older parts of Birmingham, in which the poor lived in badly-built and decrepit housing. Regarded as short, narrow and unpleasant, streets were not places that were alluring to the prosperous citizens of Birmingham.

The negative connotations of streets were recognised quickly by the leading figures of the Calthorpe Estate. In 1870 the word street was expunged from their land when Calthorpe Street, Frederick Street and George Street were renamed **Calthorpe Road**, **Frederick Road** and **George Road**. Today there are only two streets in the expanse of Edgbaston. They are **Parker Street** and **Bellis Street**, hard on the boundary with working-class Ladywood. Builders of new houses for the lower middle class and better off of the working class soon followed the example set in Edgbaston. In 1870, the Balsall Heath Local Board of Health (an independent authority until it joined Birmingham in 1891) gave permission for the cutting of **Henry Street** through the small estate of Henry Ludlow off the Ladypool Road. This was the last street to be named in that part of Sparkbrook in Balsall Heath. Twenty years later when the Watkins Estate was developed, the forming of **Brunswick Road**, **Colville Road, Fulham Road** (later **Leamington Road), Kingsley Road**, **Oldfield Road** (into which Henry Street was absorbed) and **Ombersley Road** indicated the dominance of roads.

The same pattern is apparent elsewhere. In middle-class Moseley, there are no streets – nor are there any in Acocks Green, Northfield, Selly Oak, Selly Park, Sheldon, Weoley Castle and a great collection of other outer city areas. Indeed the only streets in the outer ring are gathered around the High Street in the old village

centres – as with Erdington, Harborne and Kings Heath. Handsworth claims only a
few streets in the vicinity of **Booth Street**, whilst working-class districts built upon
from the later nineteenth century also shun streets. There are none in Alum Rock,
Bournbrook, Ward End, and Washwood Heath, all suburbanised from the 1880s
onwards; whilst Bordesley Green has only one street, **Denbigh Street**. As for Aston,
Balsall Heath, Lozells, Saltley, Small Heath and Stirchley, streets dominate the
localities closest to old Birmingham that were developed before the 1880s, and roads
characterise those parts built up from that decade.

The higher social status of roads was emphasised by Leslie Mayell in his book
The Birmingham I Remember. He stated that Sparkhill was superior to Sparkbrook
as 'For one thing it had no streets. They were all called roads.' This was a slight
exaggeration as there were six streets around **Shakespeare Street**, developed in the
1850s and well before the roads of Sparkhill. Still, there can be no dispute with
Mayell's overall impression that the address of a road gave a better impression than
that of a street. The use of lane also suffered from the prejudice of the prosperous of
Birmingham. In 1883 Ladypool Lane, Sparkbrook became known as **Ladypool
Road**, and four years later 'a resident' wrote to the *Balsall Heath Times* asserting
that, 'The postal address of Highgate Lane is bad, and has a tendency to drive away
some householders to the more congenial and pleasant sounding road'.

Ten years later **Highgate Lane** and **Thomas Street**, which was the continuation
of Highgate Lane between the Ladypool Road and the Stoney Lane, were renamed
Highgate Road. Lanes disappeared in other parts of Birmingham. In 1875 **Bear
Lane**, Edgbaston was changed to **Sandon Road**; in 1878, **Monument Lane**,
Ladywood was made Monument Road; in 1888, **Love Lane**, Sparkbrook became
known as **Medlicott Road**; in 1897 **Brick Kiln Lane**, Erdington was renamed
Summer Road and **Barrel Lane**, Handsworth was turned into **Louise Road;** and in
1898, **Workhouse Lane**, Yardley was transformed into **Holder Road**.

The rise in prominence of the word road and the prevalence of streets and lanes
in older, working-class Birmingham may well have led to the humorous Birmingham
monologue called 'The Lord Mayor Had a Coachman'. The author is unknown,
although it must have been written after 1895 when James Smith became the first
lord mayor of the city. Interestingly a Leslie Waller of Sparkbrook wrote to the
Evening Mail and stated that this monologue was a party piece of his father, whose
own father was coachman to Sir James Smith when he held office.

The Lord Mayor Had a Coachman

The Lord Mayor had a coachman and the coachman's name was John,
Said his lordship to the coachman, 'Take your wages and begone.
I want a better coachman, for I'm going to take a drive.'
Said John, 'I'm the finest coachman you will find alive.

And if you'll let me drive today I'll show I can't be beat.
I'll drive you all around Birmingham and I won't go through a street.'
Said his lordship, 'John you must be mad but still I'll humour you,
But remember that you lose your place the first street you go through.'

The mayor jumped in his carriage and the coachman on his seat,
He then drove down Victoria Road which we know is not a street,
Lozells Road, Villa Road – said his lordship, 'What's his game?'
And John drove into Soho Road and turned down Queens Head Lane,
Foundry Road and Slough Lane and Foundry Road he drives
And thus he keeps out of a street he artfully contrives.

Winson Green and Icknield Port, said his lordship, 'Well that's good',
And John wheeled round the corner into Ladywood.
Islington Row he next drives through said his lordship, 'Now he's beat.
For if you go straight on, my man, you must go through Sun Street.'
But John said, 'No that will not do, for I have another mode',
He then turned round from Lea Bank and into Ryland Road.

Charlotte Road and Wellington Road, the coachman next drives through,
Bristol Road and Belgrave Road away he quickly flew.
Now we're into Moseley Road – said his lordship in a pet –
'Dash my wig and barnacles, I think he'll do it yet.'
Highgate Place and Kyrwicks Lane and Auckland Road the same,
Stratford Road up to the Ship and then down Sandy Lane.

Coventry and Bordesley Green are the roads that next they pass.
Park Road, Mill Lane, Saltley Road through the yard they make the gas,
Then the Recreation Ground and on through Nechells Park,
Holborn Road and Lichfield Road, said his lordship, 'What a lark.'.
Said John, 'It's now Victoria Road and I think your lordship's had a treat,
For I've driven all round the city and I've not been through a street.'

The move away from the use of street and lane was accompanied by a changing of names that were thought to be unappealing. In this way **Grindstone Lane**, Edgbaston was made more acceptable as **Westfield Road** and **Hermitage Road** in 1866, whilst **Jawbone Lane**, Handsworth was turned into **Laurel Road** in 1879. In the city centre **Tonk Street** was erased for **Hill Street**, and in the outlying areas **Sheep Street**, Erdington made way for **Station Road** in 1897; **Donkey Lane**, Acocks Green was dropped for **Harvey Road** in 1906; **Tanyard Lane**, Yardley was transformed into **Amington Road** in 1907; **Madcap Lane**, Yardley became **Graham Road** in 1927; and **Bedlam Lane**, Northfield gave way to **Tessall Lane** in 1927.

Along with the vanishing of so many meaningful street names we have lost the memories inherent in a diversity of place names. Only older residents of Harborne can now bring to mind **Tom Knocker's Wood**, on the borders with Quinton and close to the meeting of the Quinton Road West and West Boulevard. In his story of old Harborne, Tom Presterne wrote that 'the wood had its terrors for the young, and for some of the old, as it was believed to be frequented by the ghost of Tom Knocker – imaginary of course. I should say that the real Tom Knocker was some night-bird, who carolling at night for his own sweet pleasure, made a peculiar noise like the tapping of a hammer – perhaps with his wings, like the pigeons do sometimes.'

Nearby in Edgbaston, until the development of the Calthorpe Estate the main hamlet was at **Good Knaves End**, located at the bottom of **Chad Hill**, also known as **Hungry Hill**, on the present **Harborne Road**. Who was the knave and why was he good – and was anyone ever hungry on the hill? It is unlikely now that we shall ever know – and nor will we find out who was the Jordan commemorated in **Jordan's Grave** in Erdington. Marked by a heap of stones close to the Chester Road, William Fowler conjectured that these stones indicated the spot 'of the last resting-place perhaps of some poor wayfarer whom nobody owned, and to whom no parish would give decent burial'. A similar explanation may be applied to the nearby **Beggars Bush**, on the borders of New Oscott and Sutton Coldfield. Local folklore tells of a beggar who died here and upon whose grave was planted a bush. But as Joe McKenna rightly stresses, such a name is not unique and refers to a place of a poor dwelling or poor soil.

In Quinton, the vividly named **Mock Beggar** or **Mopbeggar Farm** (also known as Moor End Farm and near to today's Moat Meadow) also urges us seek an explanation as to its origins. The Oxford English Dictionary states that mockbeggar applied to a house that had an appearance of wealth but was either deserted or lived in by miserly or poor persons. Shades of the Brummie phrase 'kippers and curtains'. Anthony Rosser believes that the name may have an alternative explanation. The farm was so far off the beaten track that it was a laughable to think of a beggar risking a fruitless visit there.

And what of **Bynges** in Ladywood? In 1552, King Edward VI signed a charter which set up the grammar school which carries his name still and which now is situated in Edgbaston. The new establishment was endowed with part of the possessions of the Gild of the Holy Cross, which had been dissolved during the reign of Henry VIII. The grant of lands to the school included 'all those fields, meadows and pastures, and hereditaments, whatsoever with the appurtenances, called or known by the name or names of Long-Croft, Bynges, Rotton-fields, Walmores, and Saint Mary Wood lying and being in the Foreign of Birmingham'. This ancient name Bynges was embedded in Bingley House, the home of Charles Lloyd of the banking family, and later in Bingley Hall, cleared for the International Convention Centre. The survival for so long of Bynges throws into relief the taking from our ken of field names like the **Shoulder of Mutton** which lay close to Sherlock Street and the

Horsepool Croft near to Smallbrook Street, and also of stream such as **Hersum's Dyche** or **Hassam's Ditch**. Arising from water flowing down from the fields on the slopes below where Saint Philip's now stands, the stream flowed across High Street, Moor Street and Park Street, where it was joined by another brook. The watercourse then headed down to join the River Rea, close to the 'Bull's Head', now the 'Kerryman' in Digbeth.

Many other names have disappeared, and hundreds upon hundreds of more have emerged. An understanding of the origins and location of such streets and roads enhances not only our appreciation of Birmingham's past but also an awareness of our city's place in the wider contexts of time and place. The past is not a foreign land. It is part of a continuous line running into the present and the future, informing and affecting both. If we ignore our past we cannot face the present with confidence nor can we look forward positively to the future. In a period when the cult of individuality threatens the bonds that ties us together into communities and society, the street names of Birmingham call to us to understand them and in so doing understand our collective self.

AB Row in the 1930s. Thanks to Birmingham Library Services.

A

AB Row, Duddeston

The continuation of Coleshill Street to Belmont Row, this is the shortest street name in Brum and once indicated part of the boundary between the parishes of Aston and Birmingham. For many years one of the houses in AB Row had a stone set in its front wall and on it was engraved the inscription "A+B 1764". At that time the area was part of Holte Path's Farm and an open space hereabouts was called Little Gorstey Green (see **Gosta Green**). It is likely that the stone stood on the ground until the area was developed in the late eighteenth and early nineteenth centuries. On *Pye's Map* of 1795, a house called BA is indicated opposite Duke Street but at this time AB Row was not named and instead Prospect Row ran down to Coleshill Street. It seems that AB Row itself emerged in the mid-nineteenth century as it is not shown on the 1839 'Map of the Society for the Diffusion of Useful Knowledge', but is mentioned in *White's Directory* of 1850.

The house in which the boundary stone was set was knocked down in the post-1945 redevelopment of Birmingham and the site was taken over by Gabriel and Company, whose factory had been at the rear of AB Row. This firm specialises in stainless steel products and put the stone in its front entrance. When the business was relocated the stone was handed back to the City of Birmingham. Since the development of Millennium Point, AB Row has been reduced to a short pudding bag street, a cul-de-sac. Until 1838 Deritend was also in Aston, and near to the bridge over the River Rea between Digbeth and Deritend was a building called AB House – again signifying the border between Birmingham and Aston.

Aberdeen Street, Winson Green

As Vivian Bird has shown in *Streetwise*, this brings to mind Lord Aberdeen who was Prime Minister of the United Kingdom between 1852-5. The street is obvious on Pigott Smith's Map of 1855, as is **Lansdowne Street**, named after a lord who served without office in Aberdeen's administration and who had played a part in the passage of the Great Reform Act in 1832. He is also remembered in **Landsdowne Road**, Erdington and **Lansdowne Road**, Handsworth. A Scot, Aberdeen had been Foreign Minister in Sir Robert Peel's Conservative Government of 1841-6. Both men were staunch supporters of free trade and when Peel resigned because of his support for the repeal of the Corn Laws, he was joined by Aberdeen. This connection explains the nearby **Peel Street**.

Henry John Temple, the 3rd Viscount Palmerston, also served under Aberdeen, and is remembered in **Palmerston Road**, Sparkbrook. He became prime minster in 1855, prosecuting the Crimean War with vigour, and held office until 1858. He returned to government a year later, remaining as prime minister until his death in

1865. A representative of the landowning class, he was dubbed Firebrand Palmerston because of his determined defence of British interests abroad.

A number of other streets indicate support for Liberal and reforming politicians. **Gladstone Street**, Aston, and **Gladstone Road**, Erdington, Sparkbrook and Yardley are named after William Ewart Gladstone who served as Chancellor of the Exchequer under Aberdeen and went on to become a famous Liberal prime minister, forming four governments between 1868 and 1894. His ministries brought in the Education Act of 1870 and unsuccessfully sought to bring about Home Rule for Ireland. One of Gladstone's foreign secretaries was Archibald Philip Primrose, the 5th Earl of Roseberry. For a brief time, 1895-5, he succeeded Gladstone as prime minister but led the Liberals to a defeat in the general election. Noted for his racehorses and as a biographer of British statesmen, he is brought to mind in **Rosebery Street**, Brookfields.

Beaconsfield Road, Balsall Heath, is named after Benjamin Disraeli, the leader of the Conservatives who was Gladstone's great rival. Belonging to a Sephardi Jewish family and originally a novelist, he formed two governments and was a favourite of Queen Victoria, who made him the 1st Earl of Beaconsfield. A Conservative politician is also highlighted in **Salisbury Road**, Moseley, and **Cecil Road,** Ten Acres and **Cecil Road**, Erdington (known as **Hermitage Road** until 1902). They bring to mind Robert Cecil, Marquis of Salisbury, a noted Conservative who was prime minister for the greater part of the period between 1886 and 1902. He was able to hold office for so long because of his alliance with the Liberal Unionists led by Birmingham's Joseph Chamberlain. This group had broken with Gladstone over Home Rule for Ireland and their desertion of the Liberals ended the dominance which that party had enjoyed since the passing of the Great Reform Act in 1832. (See also **John Bright Street**).

Salisbury's successor as prime minister was Arthur James Balfour, the 1st Earl, who is remembered in **Balfour Street**, Balsall Heath, so-called from 1897 when its old name of **King Street** was dropped. Balfour entered Parliament in 1874, led the Conservatives to defeat in the general elections of 1906, resigned as leader of the party in 1911 and returned to power in 1916, serving as foreign secretary under the coalition government of the First World War under Lloyd George. Perhaps he is most famous for the Balfour Declaration. Made in 1917 it promised Zionists a Jewish homeland in Palestine.

Intriguingly, the modern rump of Balfour Street is flanked by **Cobden Gardens** and **Hampden Retreat** – named after radicals who opposed conservatism. Richard Cobden was an economist and politician who is regarded as 'the apostle of free trade'. Born in the south of England he went on to be a businessman in Manchester and advocated the ending of protection so that trade could flow freely between nations. A leading figure in the Anti-Corn Law League, which sought to stop subsidies to farmers and hence Conservative landlords, he became an MP in 1846.

He was abhorred by the landed interest but was a hero to manufacturers, and nearby in Leopold Street the factory of Samuel Heath is called the Cobden Works. On the day of his funeral, 6 April 1865, there was a general closing of business in Birmingham. John Hampden was another who challenged the establishment. A lawyer and patriot, he opposed the imposition of taxes by Charles I and was a crucial figure in Parliament, leading to the emergence a Parliamentary Party oposed to the monarchy. In 1642, Charles sent troops to arrest Hampden and four others MPs and this led to the English Civil War, in which Hampden was killed fighting for the parliamentarians.

Abbey Street, Hockley

In 1799 Richard Ford, 'one of the mechanical worthies of that period' (*Showell's Dictionary*) rented waste land by Hockley Pool, also known as Boulton's Pool after Matthew Boulton. Ford employed a number of people and noticed that some of them spent their wages and time in activities which he felt was unwise. As an example to them, he put aside between twelve and fifteen shillings a week and when trade was slack instead of laying off his men he used the sum saved to pay his workers to go with horses and carts to Aston Furnace (see **Cowper Street**) for loads of slag. With this unappealing material, Ford erected a house with thick walls which was made to look like a ruined building. He called it 'Hockley Abbey' and with small pebbles set in cement he formed the figures '1473' on the front so as to add to the illusion of antiquity. The building has gone long since but is recalled in **Abbey Street**, whilst Ford himself is remembered in **Ford Street**, Hockley. Both roads run into Lodge Road.

Looking down Abbey Street, Hockley from Lodge Road in 1951.

Abbey Road, Erdington relates to Erdington Abbey on the Sutton Road. A Decorated church of sandstone it was designed by Charles Hansom for Father Daniel Haigh, a wealthy convert to Roman Catholicism. The adjoining monastery was begun in 1879 for Benedictines exiled from Germany during the time of the Chancellor Bismark. In 1922 the Benedictines returned to Germany and the monastery was taken on by the Redemptorists. The furnishings of the Abbey itself include church plate made by the famed Birmingham firm of Hardman's for Pugin, who designed Saint Chad's Cathedral; a Gothic relic chest painted by Anselm Baker that depicts scenes from the life of Saint Thomas of Canterbury; and a ring of eight bells. Today the monastery is a part of Highclare School, although the church itself (the Abbey) remains a focal point for the Catholics of Erdington.

Finally, **Abbey Road**, Harborne recalls Metchely Abbey, a large house built by about 1800 in a Gothic style. Tom Presterne, the author of *Harborne. 'Once Upon a Time'* told of one of the owners of the house, Charles Birch. He was 'one of the handsomest figures I have ever seen. He was tall and aristocratic in his bearing. He had dark curly hair and black penetrating eyes which would almost discover the innermost being of friends or enemies.' After a number of other owners, the Abbey became a ladies's school run by the Misses Howell, three sisters devoted to Wesleyan Methodism. After them the house was taken on by Sir Henry Wiggin (see Wiggin Street), who turned it into two houses.

Abbotsford Road, Sparkbrook

Abbotsford was a large house on the south side of **Anderton Road**, Sparkbrook – between Grantham Road and Cartland Road. It disappeared in the 1890s along with Green Stile Farm, which was close to Sydenham Road, and Hind's Farm and Danford Lake Farm, which were on what became **Walford Road**. The same decade saw the end of Whitmore House and its estate of sixteen acres which lay between **Whitmore Road** and **Langley Road**, Small Heath. Present since at least 1760, Whitmore House was used last as a Liberal Club. **Cyril Road** and **Henshaw Road** were cut through the Whitmore Estate.

Similarly Yew Tree House gave its name to **Yew Tree Road** Yardley; and **Endwood Court Road**, Handsworth is called after Endwood Court where the Russells lived in the early nineteenth century. **Cateswell Road**, Hall Green, **Cottesbrook Road**, Acocks Green, **Green Bank Avenue**, Hall Green, **Kingswood Road**, Moseley, **Farcroft Road**, Handsworth, and **Shaw Hill Road**, Alum Rock all bring to mind other large houses.

The fashion for naming roads after the homes of the wealthy had begun in the late eighteenth century, as was indicated by the appearance of **Lombard Street**, Deritend on part of the grounds of Lombard House. In 1807 this was described as 'very commodious', possessing two parlours, servants' rooms, six lodging rooms, cellars, stables and a garden covering half and acre. Lombard Street itself had been partly formed by 1781 when a building society put forward proposals to extend it as well as other streets close to it. (See Bradford Street and Cheapside).

Adams Hill

For centuries Woodgate was an isolated area within Northfield and by the First World War it was still a small hamlet at the bottom of Adam's Hill and at the junction with Woodgate Lane and Wood Lane. Adams Hill itself was Brook Lane until 1922.

Adderley Road, Saltley

Charles Bowyer Adderley was the first Baron Norton of Norton-in-the Moors Staffordshire. His county seat was Hams Hall, near Whitacre in Warwickshire and he was the lord of the manor of Saltley, owning the chief estates both there and in Washwood Heath. It was during his lifetime that these districts were built up and his presence is still obvious through **Adderley Road, Bowyer Road**, **Hams Road** and **Adderley Park**. This latter area of about ten acres was assigned to the city by the then Mr Adderley on a lease for 999 years at a nominal rent of five shillings a month. It was opened on 30 August 1856 and was Birmingham's first public park.

Lord Norton's mother was Anna Maria Hartopp, hence **Hartopp Road,** whilst his wife was Julia Leigh, the eldest daughter of Chandos, first Lord Leigh, thus **Leigh Road**. Other roads include first names used regularly by the Adderleys,

The corner of Adderley Street and New Bond Street in 1961.

amongst them **Ralph Road**, **Edmund Road**, **Reginald Road** and **George Arthur Road**. The latter was originally **Arthur Road**, becoming **Prince Arthur Road** in 1897. This was the year of Queen Victoria's Diamond Jubilee and there were great celebrations across the land, leading some landowners to change road names in favour of the royal family. Prince Arthur himself was the fifth child of Queen Victoria and Prince Albert and became a soldier and was made the Duke of Connaught. Four years later, the Saltley road's name was changed again to George Arthur Road.

The Adderleys gained Saltley from the Ardens in 1643 through the marriage of Sir Charles Adderley and Ann Arden (see **Arden Road**). Arden Adderley, the son of the couple, also inherited a quarter of the manor of Bordesley but sold his share to his cousins, the Bagots. This connection between Bordesley and the Adderleys led to the naming of **Adderley Street** and **Bowyer Street**.

Aerodrome Road, Castle Vale

Now gone, this road used to lead to the Castle Bromwich Aerodrome. Although named after Castle Bromwich, it lay within the ancient manor of Berwood along with parts of Minworth, Curdworth and Pype Hayes Park. Berwood had belonged to Turchill, whose descendants held the manor until it passed to the Bagots in 1643 (see Arden Road). The Bagots remained in ownership of the Castle Vale locality until 1881 when William Walter Bagot sold 344 acres of Berwood Farm to the Birmingham Tame and Rea Drainage Board, followed soon after by another 358 acres. The Drainage Board itself operated a flat, large sewage farm which ran under high cultivation to yield large crops like cabbages.

Tangmere Drive, Castle Vale in 1974. Thanks to the *Birmingham Evening Mail*.

In the early twentieth century, the development of the filtration method for treating sewage meant that less land was needed: some of it continued to be farmed; some was bought by Dunlop for their new factory; and another stretch became playing fields. In 1911, the first plane to fly over Birmingham landed on these playing fields after an aeronautical display by B. C. Hucks in a Belriot monoplane. During the First World War, the playing fields were taken over by the War Department for the Royal Flying Corps to erect hangars and workshops for a flying school. Later in the war it was a testing ground for Handley Page 0/400 and other aircraft produced locally. With the return of peace, the Castle Bromwich site as it became known was licenced as a civil aerodrome and from 1926 it was the base of No. 605 (County of Warwick) Squadron, Royal Auxiliary Air Force. Six houses built as married quarters for RAF personel can be seen still on the Chester Road, Castle Vale.

Belonging to Minworth, the Castle Bromwich Aerodrome became part of Birmingham in 1931. In the lead up to the Second World War, a shadow factory was built here for the making of planes and between 1939 and 1945 its workers made more Spitfires than any other works in the United Kingdom. Alex Henshaw, the most famous of all test pilots, was based here. By this time, 605 Aquadron had been converted to a fighter squadron and saw action in the Fall of France and the Battle of Britain. In late 1941, the Squadron was posted to the Far East where the men were caught up in the surrender to the Japanese in the Dutch East Indies (modern Indonesia).

In the 1960s, the Castle Bromwich Aerodrome area was developed by Birmingham City Council as the **Castle Vale** Estate. This name was given by Ken Roberts and Mrs H. Barker after a competition organized by the Public Works Department. Ken chose Castle because the area was in Castle Bromwich and vale because 'if you walked up the hill by the old church and looked across the airfield it was low lying' as in a vale. When the roads were cut many of them had connections with airfields. **Baginton Road, Hawkinge Drive, Drem Croft, Martlesham Square** and **Tangmere Drive**, are named after RAF stations in Warwickshire, Kent, Lothian, Suffolk and Sussex respectively and where 605 squadron was based for a time; whilst **Upavon Close, Biggin Close** and **Padgate Close** recall other RAF stations. **Dyce Close, Turnhouse Road** and **Renfrew Square** bring to mind civilian airports in Edinburgh, Aberdeen and Glasgow.

In the Scott Arms area of Great Barr and Perry Barr, there is another collection of road names connected to RAF stations. These include **Cardington Avenue, Cramlington Road, Duxford Road, Fowlmere Road, Mildenhall Road, Northolt Grove** and **Turnberry Road**; whilst **Calshot Road** is named after a sea plane base. (Thanks to Roger Henney).

There is an interesting bond between the modern and the old in Castle Vale, for it is one of the few places in Birmingham where the ancient field names have been

brought into the present through road names. The research of Geoff Bateson has
shown their survival in **Long Close Walk**, **Orchard Meadow Walk**, **Rough
Coppice Walk**, **Round Moor Walk**, and **Brook Piece Walk**, through which the
Plants Brook flowed. Field names are also harked back to in Quinton on the land
which had been Four Dwellings Farm and **Mock Beggar Farm** or **Mopbeggar
Farm**. Amongst them are **Gorsly Piece**, **Middle Leasow**, **Oak Leasow**, **Putters
Meadow** and **Rickyard Piece**.

Albert Road, various

There is an Albert Road in six districts of Birmingham: Erdington; Handsworth;
Kings Heath; Stechford; Harborne – where the road was formerly called **Wedding
Fields**; and Aston. The road in this latter district was cut out in the early 1850s and
originally was known as **Garibaldi Road**, after the Italian patriot who had been
involved in the Revolutions of 1848 which had swept Europe. Garibaldi and others
had tried to bring independence to an Italy that was dominated by the Austrians.
Similarly, the Hungarian revolutionary Louis Kossuth had sought to liberate his
people. Both revolutions failed, but on 10 November 1851 Kossuth visited
Birmingham and was greeted with tremendous enthusiasm in a place whose people
were passionate supporters of democracy. The whole town was given a holiday and
a procession of between sixty and seventy thousand men met Kossuth at Small Heath
and escorted him to Birmingham.

Garibaldi himself was invited to Birmingham in 1865, but he declined. This may
have prompted the naming of Garibaldi Road in honour of freedom fighters such as
himself. Like the other Albert Roads, it was renamed after Prince Albert, the husband
of Queen Victoria, who is also noted in **Albert Street**, City Centre and **Prince Albert
Street**, Small Heath. A German prince of the House of Saxe-Coburg and Gotha,
Albert was the first cousin of Queen Victoria and married her in 1840. Although a
dynastic union, the two fell deeply in love and Albert came to have a profound
influence over his wife and the nation.

The prince visited Birmingham on a number of occasions. In late November
1843, he stayed at Drayton Manor as a guest of the prime minister, Sir Robert Peel,
and came to Brum on the 29th of that month. After alighting at the Midland Railway
Station in Lawley Street, the royal party paid visits to the Town Hall, King Edward's
Grammar School in New Street, the Gun Barrel Proof House in Banbury Street and
a number of leading manufactories. These were the glass works of Messrs Bacchus,
the rolling mills of Messrs Muntz, the papier-maché works of Jennens and
Betteridge, the gun and sword manufactory of the Sergeant brothers, the electro-plate
works of the Elkingtons and Mr Armfield's button works.

Six years later, in September 1849, Prince Albert was drawn to Birmingham to
attend the Exhibition of Manufactures of Birmingham and the Midland Counties
which was taking place in Bingley House – then the home of the banking Lloyds (and

Albert Street in the city centre in 1961.

later the site of Bingley Hall and the ICC). The prince was impressed by what he saw. Amongst the local products on show were glass work by Osler's, stained glass from Hardman's as well as from Chance's of Smethwick, electroplated ware from Elkington's and artistic metal work by Messenger's and also Winfield's. Additionally there were exhibits of porcelain from the Potteries, carpets from Kidderminster and cotton goods from Manchester. According to Robert K. Dent, Prince Albert 'made a careful and minute examination of the various exhibits, and took copious notes, doubtless, with a view to the elaboration of the modest attempt, thus successfully carried out, which led to the Great Exhibition of 1851'. Already keen on the idea of a major exposition of Britain's manufacturing prowess, it seems that his time at Bingley House further convinced Prince Albert of the need to facilitate such a major event. As it turned out, he played an active role in the Great Exhibition of 1851, the success of which depended so much upon the manufacturing firms of Birmingham and Smethwick.

Prince Albert made two other important visits to Birmingham. First, on 22 November 1853 he laid the foundation stone for the Birmingham and Midland Insitute. This was declared by John Alfred Langford to have been 'a day of great rejoicing in the town, and was kept as a general holiday'. In his speech, Prince Albert made reference to the Great Exhibition and explained that he could not 'forget that the example of such industrial exhibitions had already been set by this town, and with the best results; or that, to the experience so acquired, the Executive Committee of the greater undertaking of '51 were much indebted in carrying out that work to a successful issue'. Finally, on 15 June 1858, Prince Albert accompanied Queen Victoria when she came to Aston Hall and Park. Tens of thousands of people greeted the royal couple on this occasion.

Despite the affection in which he was held by his wife, Albert was never really popular in the country at large. He died of typhoid on 14 December 1861 aged 42 and was lamented by Victoria for the rest of her long life. Prince Albert's funeral took place on 23 December and throughout Birmingham church bells tolled, shops were closed, curtains were drawn, flags were flown at half mast and everyone wore 'a bit of black'. Shortly afterwards a subscription list was started for a statue. It was sculpted by Mr Foley and when finished in 1867 it was placed in the Art Gallery. Made of marble it featured the prince clothed in the robes of the Order of the Bath, with a heavy cloack falling over and backwards from his shoulder. Now it stands on the main staircase in the Council House. (See also Victoria Square)

Alcester Road

It was from Alcester that John Leland approached Birmingham in 1538. He provides the first description of Birmingham and entered the town via Kings Norton, eventually coming down Camp Hill through 'as pretty a street or ever I entrd'. This was Deritend High Street, or 'Dirtey' as Leland called it.

> In it dwell smithes and cutlers, and there is a brooke that divideth this street from Birmingham, and is an Hamlett, or member belonginge to the Parish therebye (Aston).
>
> There is at the end of Dirtey a proper chappell (St John's Church) and mansion house of tymber (the 'Old Crown' pub), hard on the ripe (bank), as the brooke runneth downe; and as I went through the ford by the bridge, the water ran downe on the right hande (later Floodgate Street) and a few miles lower goeth into Tame, ripa dextra (by the right bank). This brooke riseth, as some say, four or five miles above Bermingham, towards Black Hilles.
>
> The beauty of Bermingham, a good market down in the extreame (border) parts of Warwickshire, is one street, going up alonge (Digbeth) almost from the left ripe (bank) of the brooke, up on the meane (modest) hill by the length of a quarter of a mile.

The turnpike trust for the road from Birmingham to Alcester was begun in 1753 when the stretch from Spernal Ash to Alcester was turnpiked. Fourteen years later, the section from Alcester to Digbeth was added. In 1780 Hutton described the plan of the road as tolerable, althgough it 'is rather too narrow, through a desolate country, which at present scarcely defrays the expense'. Still as many as 80 packhorses a day made their way along the Alcester Road to Birmingham's markets with garden produce from Evesham. By 1874, the whole of the road, then stretching to Evesham, had ceased to be a turnpike. Within Birmingham, the upkeep of the Alcester Road fell under the responsibility of the Council.

Alcester Street in Deritend runs parallel with the Moseley Road, which itself becomes the Alcester Road once it reaches Moseley. Until 1873, Alcester Street was called **Brewery Street**, after the Deritend Brewery, also called the Birmingham Old Brewery, on the corner of what became Alcester Street and Moseley Street. This brewery seems to have been the first large-scale concern of this kind in Birmingham and was started in 1782. The renaming of the street may be connected with the ending of the turnpike trust and of the brewery. Pronounced by Brummies of the inner city as 'Allsester' and not as 'Ulster', Alcester Street is dominated by two magnficent buildings. The first is the Roman Catholic Church of Saint Anne's, close to the junction with Bradford Street. A mission had been based here since 1849, but the church itself was built in 1884. Designed by A. Vicars in the Early English Sstyle, it is of red brick with bands of darker brick and dressings.

The second building is the Paragon Hotel. Formerly the Chamberlain Hotel, it had been opened in 1903 by Princess Alexandra as the Rowton House. A place of good quality lodgings for respectable working men who were tramping the country looking for work, the place soon deteriorated in status. My Granddad Perry stopped

The tram is approaching the terminus at Alcester Lane's End, Kings Heath in the 1920s. On the left is the 'Kings Head', better known as 'The Knob'. Thanks to Mary Allthorpe.

there for a night as a young lad of fourteen when he he had to leave home. Despite its loss of prestige, the Rowton House continued to be of importance, providing lodgings for many Irish chaps who came to work in Birmingham during the Second World War. From the 1950s onwards its name was changed to the Alexandra Hotel and the Highgate Hotel and after it was closed, two local entrepreneurs refurbished it. The hotel now belongs to a Singapore based group.

Alfred Street, Aston and Sparkbrook

There is an **Alfred Road** in Handsworth and another in Sparkhill, whilst there is an Alfred Street in four other districts: Handsworth; Kings Heath; Aston and Sparkbrook. The Aston street may be named after Alfred Taylor, a county councillor for Aston and a chairman of Aston Local Board of Health, the body which ran Aston before it became a borough; whilst the Sparkbrook street recalls Alfred East. He was the son of the Reverend Timothy East, minister of the Ebenezer Chapel in Steelhouse Lane between 1818-43. East was influential in setting up Spring Hill College (see **College Road**) for the training of Congregational ministers, and was a popular preacher. He left the chapel following disputes over his commercial undertakings which supposedly put 'his reputation at peril'. It may be that these undertakings were property deals, for the first houses in Alfred Street, Sparkbrook were built in 1845, soon after he left the chapel.

All Saints Road, Kings Heath

This takes its name from All Saints Church, Kings Heath. Built in 1859, its architect was F. Preedy, who designed the church in the Perpendicular style with a chancel, knave, aisles and tower with a spire. The parish of All Saints was assigned out of the parishes of Saint Nicolas, Kings Norton and Saint Mary's, Moseley. **All Saints Street**, Brookfields and Hockley and **All Saints Road**, Hockley refer to a a Gothic style church designed by Ritchman and Hutchinson and consecrated in 1833. A year later a parish was assigned out of Saint Martin's in the Bull Ring.

Allens Cross, Northfield

A part of Northfield, this area is mentioned in a document of 1631, whilst another deed for 1690 notes the presence of a cross. The present Allens Cross council estate was built during the inter-war years. On 2 September 1931, the first community hall erected on a Corporation Housing Estate was opened at Allens Cross by George Cadbury.

Alum Rock Road

Alum Rock is one of the most mysterious of Birmingham's place names. Some stories state that it goes back to the time at the ended of the nineteenth century when Southall's set up a manufactory on the Alum Rock Road for the making of surgical

Tenants at Allens Cross, Northfield taking part in a rent strike march through the streets in April 1939. The strike arose from a rent rise by the Council and the imposition of a means test on those who could not pay their rents. Women led the way in this protest, organising socials, trips and a mock funeral to bury the bailiff – because the Council sent in bailiffs. Despite such action against them, the rent strikers won the day. Thanks to the *Birmingham Evening Mail*.

dressings. The company dug an artesian well, thus finding alum rock – from which comes a thin-bedded material a whitish and translucent mineral salt. Such an interpretation poses a problem because in 1759 John Tomlinson drew a map of Little Bromwich, of which much of modern Alum Rock was a part, and noted the Allum Rock Estate. Its farm buildings and house were on the Alum Rock Road just up from the junction with Cotterills Lane, and the estate was bounded to the north by the Slade Field, remembered in **Sladefield Road**, and to the west by Brokhill, hence **Brokhill Road**.

Another document dated 1718 also mentions an Alom Rock. Still, Southall's is almost opposite the Brookhill and perhaps the Allum Rock Estate itself was named after the salt mineral. Intriguingly, the 1894 King's Norton Map includes a fulminate factory just off Cotterrills Lane and directly to the east of the estate. Fulminate is the term used for any of a number of unstable explosive salts of metals and used in detonators. As late as Bacon's Map of Birmingham in 1882, the road was named the **Coleshill Road**.

A rural Alum Rock Road at the turn of the twentieth century.

Alvechurch Road, West Heath

Obviously this is the road leading to Alvechurch, itself mentioned in a document of 780 and meaning Aelfgythe cyrce – the church founded by a woman called Aelfgythe.

Alwold Road, Weoley Castle

The Norman Conquest was the most traumatic event in the history of England. Following the victory of William the Conqueror over King Harold at the Battle of Hastings, the lands of those Anglo-Saxon thegns who had fought with their king were taken. Over the next twenty years, more land passed out of the control of the Anglo-Saxons following rebellions and the flight of leading lords. By the time of the Domesday Book in 1086 over 90% of England was owned by supporters of William and who had come from northern France. In Warwickshire, however, Turchill de Arden maintained a strong presence (see **Arden Road**), and a number of other Anglo-Saxons continued to hold land. They included Godmund of Aston and Stannnachetel of Witton, whose overlord was William FitzAnsculf. Nothing else is known about these two men and their families. Elsewhere the evidence of first names would suggest that Normans took over the manors in and around Birmingham. In Northfield the lord of the manor was William, although in 1066 it had been held by Alfwold. This Anglo-Saxon who was dispossesed is recalled in **Alwold Road**.

Ceolmund Crescent, Chelmsley Wood is another rare example of a street named after an Anglo-Saxon. Part of Solihull since the local government reorganization of 1974, Chelmsley Wood was taken from Coleshill and developed from the late 1960s by Birmingham City Council with municipal homes for Brummies. We know nothing of Ceolmund, except that his name is brought to mind in Chelmsley Wood, which means the wood of Ceolmund – and the area was first mentioned around 1200 as the wood called Chelemundesheia. It remained a beautiful rural spot for hundreds of years and many Brummies recall fondly cycling to the bluebell woods at Chelmsley Wood. Much of the estate is filled with roads named after trees, but **Bacons End** recalls a farm which was recorded on a rental of 1447 at the north-western tip of the wood.

Amington Road, Acocks Green

Known as **Tanyard Lane** till 1907, this was named after the Yardley Tannery started by George Muscott in 1884. His company continued making high quality shoe leather until the mid-1960s. As with all tanyards, the smell was strong and unappealing. Consequently, Tanyard Lane may have given negative impressions so that the name was changed to Amington Road, after a large house on the road.

Anderton Road, Sparkbrook

Anderton's farm in Sparkbrook was originally known as Green Stile Farm and belonged to the Taylors of Moseley Hall. It then came into the tenancy of Thomas Anderton, after whom the road (originally the lane) was called. The farmhouse was on the corner of what is now **Fallows Road** and Anderton Road. The farmland was developed by the Barber Trust after the death of Anderton in 1896. Henry Barber was a wealthy Birmingham solicitor and it was his wife who endowed the Barber Institute of Fine Arts at The University of Birmingham.

Anderton Park Road, Moseley

During the nineteenth century the Anderton family was one of the most prominent in Moseley. (It is not known if they were related to Thomas Anderton of Sparkbrook, see Anderton Road). They owned 596 acres in the district and lived in a grand house in **Belle Walk**, purportedly named after one of the daughters of a William Anderton and known formerly as **Gilden Corner Road**. After their father's death, the Misses Anderton became noted benefactors, giving money both for the building of a house for the vicar of All Saints, Kings Heath and for much of church itself. Rebecca Anderton also paid for the construction of St Anne's, Park Hill at a cost of over £6,000. The family estate was sold in 1877 and new roads were cut through it. Most of them have a connection with trees, as with **Coppice Road** and **Chestnut Road**, or else with woods, as with **Queenswood Road** and **Forest Road**.

Anderton Square, City

In or about 1775, Isaac Anderton a toymaker built a square named after him off Whittall Street. Houses occupied three sides of the cobbled square and a clock was placed on the central gable on a large detached house that occupied the west side, leading to the square becoming known as **Clock Dial Yard**. It was here in 1782 that John Wesley stayed. The followers of this great religious leader later formed the Methodist Church. On this particular occasion Wesley preached at the 'dreary old preaching-house', as he described it in his journal, in an old theatre in Moor Street. He stayed in Anderton Square with a family called Newey and held meetings in their home. The Neweys were Huguenots, French Protestants who fled to England to escape persecution. Members of the family lived in Anderton Square from the 1770s until as late as 1903. The square later became part of the premises of Parker Hale Ltd but was cleared in the 1960s.

Ansell Road, Erdington

Born in 1841 at Gosta Green, where his father was a maltster, Joseph Ansell became intimately associated with Aston after his family moved there and became major brewers of beer. It was said of him that if he were taken out of the local life of Aston Manor then 'you take away the man who has been the guiding spirit of that life ever since the Manor had an individuality of its own to assert'. A solicitor in Waterloo Street, when the Aston Local Board of Health was formed in 1869. Ansell became its legal adviser. In the following years he played a prominent role in the campaigns to obtain a Member of Parliament for Aston and for the district to be incorporated as a borough. From 1880, Ansell lived at Wylde Green and he became deputy mayor of Sutton Coldfield for three years in a row. Ansell Road itself is in Erdington, which belonged historically to the parish of Aston.

Arden Road, Saltley

The Adderleys (Adderley Road) gained Saltley through the marriage of Sir Charles Adderley and Anne Arden, hence **Arden Road**. She was the youngest of the four sisters of Robert Arden, who died heroically fighting for the Royalists in 1643 in the English Civil War. He was the last male in the direct line of one of the most ancient families in England. The Ardens were descended from the Anglo-Saxon lord, Wulfwine (or Ulwine as the Normans spelled it) who owned wide lands in Warwickshire and was the nephew of Leofric, Earl of Mercia, and Lady Godiva, who founded the Benedictine priory that was responsible for the growth of Coventry. Presumably because he did not fight at the Battle of Hastings in 1066, Wulfwine was allowed to keep the great majority of his estates in north Warwickshire. These included Park Hall, Castle Bromwich, Peddimore, Sutton Coldfield, Curdworth and Minworth. Wulfwine's son, Turchill, took the surname Arden in the late 1080s. He is recalled in **Turchill Drive**, Walmley.

Amongst the many possessions of the Ardens was the manor of Berwood, which included Castle Bromwich and the modern Castle Vale – hence **Berwood Road** (named as **Bridge Road** in 1804), **Berwood Gardens** and **Berwood Farm Road** by

Pype Hayes Park off the Chester Road, and **Berwood Lane**, Pype Hayes. Berwood came into the hands of the Bagots in 1643 through the marriage of Dorothy Arden, another of Robert's sisters, to Sir Hervey Bagot, leading to **Hervey Grove** by Pype Hayes Park. (See also Pype Hayes Road).

The Ardens themselves had their main home at Park Hall and came into possession of Saltley through the marriage of an earlier Robert Arden with Elizabeth, the heiress of the Clodeshale family (see Clodeshall Road). This Robert was the first Yorkist to be executed in the Wars of the Roses (at Ludlow in 1452) – for raising troops for his Earl, Richard Neville, the Earl of Warwick known as the 'Kingmaker'. His son, Walter, is shown in a stained glass window in Aston Parish Church with his wife, Elizabeth Hampden. Their son, John, fell in love with Alice Bracebridge of Kingsbury and according to folklore floated love letters to her on the River Tame. The Bracebridges also claimed Turchill as an ancestor, but Walter Arden disapproved of the relationship. Alice's father was so upset at his daughter's pining that he and his followers kidnapped John and eventually, Walter Arden agreed to the marriage in 1474. Both male Ardens and many of their descendants are buried in Aston Parish Church. It is believed that John's younger brother, Thomas, inherited the Arden property at Wilmcote near Aston Cantlow and was the grandfather of Mary Arden, the mother of William Shakespeare.

Armoury Road, Small Heath

In 1862 work was finished on the Birmingham Small Arms Company factory in a green-field site on the borders of Small Heath with Sparkbrook and Greet. The business had been set up by a number of leading manufacturers who recognised the need to bond together to challenge the Royal Enfield works which was owned by the government and had been producing guns since 1858. Before the BSA, gun-making in Birmingham was workshop based in the Gun Quarter and was characterised by a marked division of labour. The BSA factory brought gunmakers together under one roof and led to quicker manufacturing techniques for mass produced guns. The 26 acre site of the new works was well placed for communications as it was close to the line of the Great Western Railway and the Birmingham and Warwick Canal. Armoury Road was so named because of the arms made by the BSA – although in the twentieth century the firm also became famous for its motor bikes.

Arter Street, Balsall Heath

Mary E. Allthorpe tells me that this street in Balsall Heath was named after Mr Arter of Daniel and Arter. The partners operated the Globe Nevada Silver Works in Upper Highgate Street and made spoons. Interestingly, Sorrento House on the Wake Green Road, Moseley – later a maternity hospital – was built by Mr Daniels as a wedding present for his wife. Developed in the 1830s, Arter Street was originally **Mount Pleasant** and was renamed in 1897.

Ashley Passage, City

The cutting of Corporation Street from the later 1870s to the end of the century (see Corporation Street) led to the clearing of some of the worst slum properties in Birmingham. Amongst them were the buildings in **The Gullett**. This was an infamous street which supposedly was filled with ruffians and villains. In reality, its people were amongst the poorest in the city and were mostly widows, children and the elderly. However, the negative image of The Gullett suited the purposes of the supporters of the Corporation Street Improvement Scheme, for it allowed them to gain support for the need to sweep away 'dens of vice' so close to the Council House and the middle-class shopping thoroughfare of Bull Street.

The Gullett did not completely disappear and part of it was called Ashley Passage. Joe McKenna believes that both names were derived from a former owner of the land, Ashley Gullett. I feel that The Gullett was so called because it was narrow like the Gullett in the human body. Before the 1830s, The Gullett was known as **The Ditch**. It is shown thus on Westley's Map of 1731 and it ran from Coleshill Street to the junction of Vauxhall Street, Lichfield Street, Aston Street, Lancaster Street and Steelhouse Lane.

Ashold Farm Road, Erdington

One of three farms in Bromford Meadows, Ashold Farm may mean Ash Hole Farm. It dates back to at least the early eighteenth century, becoming a sewage farm of Birmingham City Council in the early 1900s. The city drains through four main valleys, those of the River Tame and its tributaries the Rivers Rea and Cole and the Hockley Brook. Each of these valleys has a main sewer and in the early twentieth century they discharged into four farms of which Ashold was one. The others were at Saltley, Yardley and Acocks Green. Ashold Farm was owned by the Rumbles and when it was taken on by the Corporation, John Scott Rumble became the farm bailiff. From the mid-1920s, the building of new factories began to claim the agricultural land locally and later the sewage works were transferred to Minworth. The farmhouse remained close to the Fort Dunlop entrance. (See also Aerodrome Road).

Ashted Row, Ashted

Originally part of Sir Lister Holte's estates in Duddeston (see Holte Road), Ashted is named after Dr John Ash. He was a well-respected physician who became a noted figure in Birmingham and was the driving force in the opening of the General Hospital in 1769. Completed ten years later, this facility was in the Summer Lane neighbourhood and led to the appearance of **Hospital Street**. The General moved from this locality to Steelhouse Lane in 1897. A wealthy man, Ash decided to buy land from Holte and to lay out it out as a new district. Notices to this effect appeared in 1788 and at first the new area was known as Ashstead – the (home)stead of Ash. Later the 'a' from stead was dropped and the area became known as Ashted. The main road in the district was

Ashted Row in 1956. Thanks to the *Birmingham Evening Mail*.

Ashted Row, originally called **Mile End, Ashted**, and it was graced with elegant Georgian buildings. Many doctors lived in Ashted Row until, sadly, its buildings were knocked down in the post-Second World War redevelopment of Birmingham.

Ash himself moved to London soon after development began on his estate and it was leased by an attorney called Brookes, hence **Great Brook Street** (although what happened to the 'e' from Brooke is a mystery). He sought to lay out Ashted as an attractive suburb, the focal point of which was Ash's home which became the chapel of Saint James. Birmingham's first historian, William Hutton, declared that Brookes was a 'hungry attorney' and he became a notorious figure during the riots of 1791 when mobs of loyalist Brummies attacked and plundered the homes of wealthy Non-Conformists who were thought to be supporters of the French Revolution – a grave charge when Britain was at war with revolutionary France (see Priestley Road). Brookes and another magistrate called Carless were regarded as key figures in fomenting the disorder (see also Carless Avenue). It is said that Brookes gained a fortune but lost it in building speculation. He died in 1801. During the riots, one of his tenants called William Windsor was fearful that his property in Ashted would be destroyed because he was supposedly not loyal. On 16 July 1791 Brookes sent out a notice declaring that Windsor was a 'real true blue'. He gave his name to **Windsor Street** which in the later ninteenth and twentieth centuries became well known for its gas works.

Aston Brook Street, Aston

The Hockley Brook provided the boundary between Birmingham and Handsworth and part of the border between Birmingham and Aston. A small stream, it becomes known as the Aston Brook when it enters the old manor of Aston just beyond Hockley Hill. It eventually runs into the River Rea (see Rea Street) at Nechells.

Aston Church Road, Washwood Heath and Nechells

In the Middle Ages, Aston Parish was a great size and included what is now Ashted, Bordesley, Bordesley Green, Deritend, Duddeston, much of Gosta Green, Highgate, Little Bromwich, Nechells, Saltley, Ward End, Washwood Heath and Vauxhall. At that time, it was the law that folk had to worship on a Sunday, but the wide extent of Aston meant that it was a trip of miles for many folk to reach the parish church of Saint Peter's and Saint Paul's, which lay then as now close to the modern Villa Park. The journey was made more difficult for the people of the manors of Saltley and Little Bromwich because they had to cross the River Rea. As a result, by the 1400s they had a bridge put up which allowed them to travel more easily. The route which led to this crossing became known first as **Church Road** and then as **Aston Church Road** in 1895.

The parish of Saint Peter's and Saint Paul's probably dates to before the Norman Conquest, as in the Domesday Book of 1086 there is mention of a priest at Aston. A stone building, its tower is from the fifteenth century, although the rest of the church is more modern. The spire was put up in 1776 and the rest of the building between 1879 and 1890. At the west end of the nave are four choir stalls from the late fifteenth century, whilst there are a large number of ancient monuments. The church also boasts an Erdington Chantry, founded in 1449 when Sir Thomas Erdington, lord of Erdington Manor, was granted a licence for a chaplain to celebrate divine service at the altar of Saint Mary the Virgin. **Church Lane** and **Church Road**, Aston also refer to Aston Parish Church.

Aston Cross, Aston

This is so named because it is the cross-roads of **Park Lane**, **Park Road,** the **Aston Road North,** the **Lichfield Road** and **Rocky Lane** and because it was dominated from 1853 by a clock tower. Bill Ainsworth's research has revealed that this spot was known as **Catchem's End** and that the name Aston Cross did not come into general use until the gates to Aston Park – then in various stages of development – were removed in 1862. The first clock was put up by a builder called Heritage who bought many of the plots of land around Aston Cross and who wanted to draw attention to his developments through an eye-catching focal-point. Later given to the Aston Board of Health, the clock became unsafe and was demolished in 1891 to be replaced by the present clock. It is probable that **Tower Road** was named after original and large clock which looked like a tower.

Aston Hall Road

The continuation of Waterworks Street, Aston Hall Road now runs under the Aston Expressway, in front of Aston Parish Church to its junction with Witton Lane, opposite which is Aston Hall and Park. The hall itself was built under the orders of Sir Thomas Holte, who was created a baronet in 1611. He commenced the construction in 1618 and moved there in 1631. King Charles 1 was entertained in Aston Hall on his way to Shrewsbury to relieve Banbury Castle in 1642 and in the December of the following year, the Parliamentarians of Birmingham attacked Sir Thomas and his force of 40 musketeers. He surrendered after three days and the marks of cannon shot can be seen still on the walls and balusters of the Great Staircase.

The Holtes lived in the hall until the death of Dame Sarah Holt, the widow of Sir Lister, when the property passed to the Honourable Heneage Legge, the nephew of Sir Lister's first wife, (see Holte Road and Legge Street). In 1818 it was bought by a firm of Warwick bankers who leased it to James Watt the younger, the son of the celebrated engineer. He lived there until 1848, after which the greater part of the estate was sold off for building and the herd of deer was sold. For a time there was concern about the survival of the hall and the remnant of the park. In 1856 it was bought by a private company formed expressly to save Aston Hall and two years later, Queen Victoria came to open the hall and park.

Looking down the Aston Road North towards Aston Cross and the Ansell's Brewery in the late 1950s. On the right is the old Astoria Picture house, later the Alpha Television Studios.

Then, in 1863, a woman tight-rope walker was sadly killed at a fete and the Queen wrote to the Mayor of Birmingham angry that 'one of her subjects – a female – should have been sacrificed to the gratification of the demoralising taste'. Another letter from the monarch expressed surprise that Birmingham should have difficulty in buying the hall and shamed into action, the Council acquired Aston Hall and Park. It is now a public park and museum. (See also Holte Road and Rupert Street). Today Aston Hall is acknowledged as one of the finest Jacobean mansions in the country, made distinctive by its two wings and its long gallery.

Aston Road North, Aston

As it suggests, this road is the continuation of the older Aston Road, Birmingham which ran from the end of Corporation Street, by Bagot Street. One of the most notable residents of the Aston Road North was Arthur Conan Doyle. He practised as a doctor between 1878-1881 at number 63, before he became famous as the creator of Sherlock Holmes. His home lay between Avenue Road and Holland Road and is indicated by a plaque put up by the Birmingham Civic Society.

Asylum Road, Summer Lane

An asylum for poor children was founded in 1797 and sited in the Summer Lane neighbourhood. It was supported from the poor rate and could accommodate 343 boys and girls. It was closed and dismantled in 1846, but the name Asylum Road continued in use. Before the building was put up, this road was called **Bread Lane**.

Austin Street, Nechells

Formerly Ann Street and becoming Austin Street in 1872, the date of the renaming is too early too suggest that it relates to Austen Chamberlain, the oldest son of Joseph Chamberlain, who was only nine years old at the time. Whatever its origins, Austin Street ran from Nechells Park Road to Mount Street and was one of a host of streets to disappear in the post-Second World War redevelopment of Birmingham. Some others included **Blythe Street**, Ladywood, off Ledsam Street and which was **Chester Street** until 1887; **Don Street**, Winson Green, known as **Mount Street** until 1887; **Ashley Street**, that ran between Wrentham Street and Benacre Street and which was called **Nelson Street South** until 1887; and **Cranbury Street**, Nechells, named **Smith Street** until 1897.

B

Bacchus Road, Handsworth

Bacchus was the Greek God of wine, yet Bacchus Road is named not after him but after George Bacchus. In 1818, Wrightson's Directory noted the Union Glass Works of Bacchus, Green and Green in Dartmouth Street, Ashted; however, Bacchus was more than a businessman. He was one of Birmingham's leading citizens and in the 1830s he played a prominent role in pushing for rail links with Liverpool and London, serving on the committees of both projects. Originally Bacchus Road was called **Gibb Heath Road**, after a locality which is shown on the Birmingham A to Z, but which has not been familiar to Brummies for generations. It lay to the north east of Winson Green and covered the land between the Birmingham to Wolverhampton railway and the Hockley Brook. In effect, it included the district through which struck Park Road and it was bounded to the north by Benson Road and Factory Road and to the south by Norton Street.

Bagot Street, City

Sir Lister Holte (see Holte Road) owned great estates in the wide parish of Aston and when he died without issue he left his property to his brother Charles – upon the death of whom the lands were to go in succession to the nephews of his first wife, Lady Anne Legge. They were Heneage Legge and Lewis Bagot, Bishop of Saint Asaph. If they died without issue the estates were to go to Wriothesley Digby of Meriden Hall (see Digby Walk). This Lewis Bagot is recalled in Bagot Street, which started at Princip Street and went into the bottom end of Corporation Street as it met the Aston Road. The Bagots were also connected with Erdington. (See also Adderley Road, Arden Road and Pype Hayes Road).

The back-to-backs of Number 4 Court in Bagot Street at the turn of the twentieth century.

Bailey Street

This used to go between Lancaster Street and Loveday Street and was named before 1772 after a landowner called Bayliss. It changed from **Bayliss Street** to Bailey Street in the early nineteenth century and disappeared with the cutting of the Saint Chad's Queensway in the 1960s.

Baker Street, Small Heath and Sparkhill

George Baker belonged to one of the longest-established families of Friends (Quakers) in Birmingham. His great grandfather, Samuel, was one of the first men on the town's Street Commission – the body which provided a limited form of local government before Birmingham gained a council in 1838 (see also Barker Street). George Baker himself was elected a councillor in 1868 and was later an alderman, becoming mayor in 1876-7. He was active in the Finland Famine Fund and taught at the famous Severn Street Schools, where Friends and Unitarians gave their time freely to help working men to improve their education.

Bagshaw Road, Stechford

Val Robinson tells me that for many years Frank Bagshaw was a councillor for the Stechford area and when a new estate was built locally 'the Council decided to have one of the roads named after him, for all the work he had done'. Frank also fought to get Stechford Baths opened.

Balden Road, Harborne

A continuation of Court Oak Road, Balden Road was named in 1897 after Mr E. H. Balden, the agent for the Calthorpe Estate. It seems likely that he was related to the Baldens who owned land in both Harborne and Balsall Heath in the nineteenth century. **Heaton Road**, cut in the mid 1950s, was called after Guy Heaton, the man who succeeded Mr Balden as agent in 1925.

Baldwin Road, Kings Norton

Born in 1800, James Baldwin came to Birmingham as a teenager. He worked at a printer's, saved a sufficient sum of money and became an employer by the age of 25. In the early years, he had a patent gun wadding and sugar mill manufactory in Newhall Street and a paper manufactory in Morville Street, Ladywood, whilst he lived in Kings Norton. Later on, he focused production at Sherbourne Mill, Kings Norton where his firm also made paper and paper bags. In particular, he specialised in grocery printing. Baldwin was a prominent figure locally in the campaign against the 'tax on knowledge' – this was the Stamp Acts which required the payment of a stamp on each single newspaper and pamphlet. Obviously, this law caused a drastic increase in the cost of such printed material, badly affecting not only the spread of democratic views but also the economic viability of the printing trade. The stamp was reduced to one penny in 1836 and the measure was abolished in 1855. Baldwin himself became a councillor and an alderman and was mayor in 1853. He settled at a farm near to his mills and died in 1871.

Ballon Street, Gun Quarter

A short street off Brick Kiln Street, itself coming from Lancaster Street, this may commemorate an event on 31 January 1785 when a Mr Harper was the first person to rise up above Birmingham in a balloon. His made his ascent from the Tennis Courts in Coleshill Street, not far from Balloon Street, and is said to have gone a distance of 57 miles in 80 minutes. It is believed that the first Primitive Methodist Chapel in Birmingham was started in Balloon Street in 1826. The street was cleared in 1882 as part of the Corporation Street Improvement Scheme.

Balsall Heath Road, Balsall Heath

Balsall Heath was first mentioned in 1541 as Bordishalle Hath and according to W.B. Bickley, an expert on this area, it was the place in the hollow owned by a man called Bord. He felt that it was associated with Bordesley, which adjoined Balsall Heath. Bickley explained that locally folk did not pronounce the 'd' in Bordesley, thus Bordishalle Heath became Bor'shalle Heath. By 1753, the name was spelt as Balsall Heath. The heath itself stretched from the Spark Brook to the Moseley Road, below which were fields on the slopes leading down to the River Rea.

Balsall Heath Road was cut across these fields as 'the grand new road' in 1829, following the bankruptcy of William Moore who owned the Frowd or Moore Estate. With the agreement of the owners of Edgbaston, a bridge was put across the River Rea so that the Balsall Heath Road could link the Moseley Road with the Pershore Road. This remained the only crossing point on the Rea for carriages between Digbeth and Edgbaston Lane until the bridge over Edward Road was built in 1899.

Bank Alley, City

Named after the original bank, the 'Old Bank' of Lloyd's on the edge of High Street and Dale End, this alley went to Moor Street and was demolished in 1882.

Bargehouse Walk, Hawkesley

Going parallel with Edgewood Road and Thatchway Gardens, Vivian Bird notes that this walk is almost above the Wast Hill Tunnel on the Birmingham and Worcester canal. The barge horses would be led over the tunnel whilst the narrow boats themselves were legged by the boatmen through the tunnel.

Barker Street, Ladywood and Lozells

George Barker was a prominent lawyer and Conservative and was a key figure in the opposition to Birmingham becoming an incorporated borough with an elected council. The campaign for incorporation sprang up during 1837-8. At that time, the only form of local government was the Street Commission, set up in 1769 with authority to widen certain ways and cleanse and light the streets. An unelected group of wealthy citizens, the commissioners themselves chose people for vacancies and gained more powers in 1773. Despite their oligarchic nature, they were responsible for major improvements, paying for the Town Hall and the old Market Hall and causing the demolition of property to open up the Bull Ring into a great triangular space.

Still, following on from the movement for Parliamentary reform, supporters of democracy pushed for an elected council. Barker and his fellows felt that there was no need for such a body, arguing that the town's success had arisen because it was not incorporated. They lost the argument and Birmingham became a municipal borough in 1838. Barker's various homes included Bellefield, hence **Bellefield Street**, Winson Green, and Springfield, thus **Springfield Street**, Spring Hill, which is not far from Barker Street, Ladywood. He also owned land in Aston, which led to **Barker Street**, Lozells. A lawyer to the Colmores (see Colmore Row), Barker was also noted as a collector of coins and of rare orchids .

Barnes Hill, Weoley Castle
In the early 1800s John Barnes was a brickmaster in this locality.

Barnes Hill Shopping Centre at Weoley Castle, 1930s.

Barrack Street, Ashted
Following the Church and King Riots of 1791 (see Ashted Row and Priestley Road) when the town suffered from the want of immediate aid from the army, the government leased five acres of land from Heneage Legge in Duddeston (see also

Holte Road). These barracks had space for 162 men and horses and were erected in 1793. They disappeared in the 1930s and were replaced by the council with the Ashcroft Estate.

Barrows Road, Sparkbrook

This road may be called after Joseph Barrows, J.P. He was prominent in public life as a Guardian of the Poor and was one of Street Commisioners who transferred the powers of that body to the corporation in 1851. A partner in an iron and coal business with his brother-in-law, Frederick Welch of Moseley, and the founder of a wine merchants named after him, he was a Conservative and strong supporter of the Church of England. A justice of the peace for Worcestershire, Barrows sat at Balsall Heath and Kings Heath and lived in Yardley – all of which were part of Worcestershire until 1911.

Bartholomew Street

Along with **Bartholomew Row** and **New Bartholomew Street**, this street takes its name from Saint Bartholomew's Church. Built in 1749, it was a chapel at ease for Saint Martin's, hence the nearby **Chapel Street**; that is, it was an easier church to travel to for people who lived distant from the parish church of Birmingham in the east of the town. The site was given by John Jennens, a wealthy local ironmaster (see Jennens Row), whose wife handed over £1,000 towards the building itself. The rest of the money was raised by public subscription When it was first opened for worship, it was on the skirts of the built up part of Brum and was placed on what had been arable land. By the early years of the nineteenth century, it was in the midst of a populous working-class neighbourhood and in 1847, Saint Bartholomew's became a parish church. It was demolished by 1943.

From the 1880s until soon after the Second World War, these streets and **Duddeston Row** were known collectively as Birmingham's Italian Quarter. Duddeston Row itself was a short street that led, as it suggests, from Birmingham to Duddeston. It used to stretch between Curzon Street and Albert Street, within the latter of which it is now included. The majority of Birmingham's Italians came from the commune of Picinisco, in the province of Caserta, which was part of Campania in Naples. This area lies between Montecassino to the south and Sora to the north. In particular, the Nobladani, as they were known, hailed from the communes of Atina and Gallinaro and the village of Carnello. The pioneers of this migration seem to have been members of the Delicata family.

In 1881 a Guiseppe Delicata, a street musician, was living at the back of 33, Bartholomew Street. His wife, Maiscatta, was nineteen and their fifteen-month old son had been born in Birmingham. Fifteen street musicians lodged with them, of whom fourteen were Italian and one was English. Amongst them was Antonia Frezza, whose family live still in Birmingham. In 1885, a Domenico Delicata

The 'Park House' a hostel for men is on the corner of Fox Street and Duddeston Row, which goes up towards Masshouse Lane and Albert Street, about 1949.

witnessed the marriage of Lucia Capoti and Gerarde Abrezese, whose descendants also remain locally. Six years later, a Delicata was giving lodgings to three members of the Volante family – again still present in the city. Nearby lived more Volantes and Antonio and Antonia Tavolier. The birth of Antonio in Atina had been registered by a Guiseppe Delicata in 1863. Antonia Tavolier herself was a Bove, and she provided the bridgehead for other members of her family to join her.

Through the chain migration of kin, Birmingham's Italians were tight-knit, but within a generation they were intermarrying with local English and Irish families. Still, the Italian Quarter had a distinctive feel. The Albericcis made the barrel organs hired out by the Secondinis and others. The Tamburros played and hired accordions. The Iommis, Zacarinis, Tersignes and more made wonderful yellow ice cream. The Mattiellos constructed ice cream conservators. The Facchinos produced ice cream wafers and cones. The Bastianellis, De Felices and Barlones sold Italian provisions. And the Mieles and others worked for northern Italian terraza contractors such as the Panicalis. The Italians, like other immigrants, made a deep and lasting mark upon Birmingham, and indeed one of them, Martin Ciangretta, cleared the land for the building of the Hall of Memory. The Italian Quarter lost its feel with the post-war redevelopment and the desire of second and third generation Brummie Italians to live in better housing.

Barton Street, Aston

On the 1758 Map of Aston by John Tomlinson there is a Barton's Close and a Barton's Wood, presumably named after a local person. Barton Street itself was **Fordrough**, Aston until 1881 and gave its name to the Barton's Arms on High Street, Aston. This is the most spectacular late Victorian pub in Birmingham and is one of the finest in the world. Distinguished by its snob screens at the bar, its wonderful windows and superb tiled scenes, it was the drinking place for many of the stars who performed at the Aston Hippodrome just across the way.

Baskerville Place, City

Originally, Baskerville Place ran between Cambridge Street and Broad Street. It was cleared in 1927 for the building of Baskerville House and the Hall of Memory. The name was then given to a passage running alongside King Alfred's Place and opposite the Registry Office in Broad Street. Like King Alfred's Place, Baskerville Passage was removed for the building of the International Convention Centre and Centenary Square.

John Baskerville himself was one of a select group of manufacturers who gained fame for Birmingham as a manufacturing centre in the eighteenth century. Born in 1706 in Wolverley, Worcestershire, he had come to Brum as a young man. At first he earned his living by inscribing gravestones and by teaching others to write in Edgbaston Street. Then, about 1740, he set up as a japanner in Moor Street and was acclaimed as bringing about an entire revolution in the making of goods which became black and glossy through the application of a hard varnish. Becoming a wealthy man, Baskerville built a splendid house on Easy Hill (see Easy Row) where Baskerville House now stands. This was a 'little Eden' for him and his wife Sarah, one of the wealthy Rustons, hence **Ruston Street**, Ladywood.

At Easy Hill, Baskerville turned his mind to his passion, the art of writing, and created an incomparable form of type for printing. It is said that he spent £600 before he had made a single letter to please him. Baskerville also made his own paper, prepared his own ink, worked on his own presses and probably bound some of his own books. He was visited by Benjamin Franklin, the great American statesman, writer and scientist who praised his type. In the words of Samuel Timmins, one of the early historians of Birmingham, 'great as the triumphs of the art of printing have been, and numerous as are the laurels which Birmingham has won, there are few nobler chapters in our local story than those which record how . . . in a material and commercial age, John Baskerville made our town famous throughout the civilised world for the production of the best and greatest works of man, in a style which has rarely been equalled, and even now, has never been surpassed'.

A lover of colourful clothes who was often seen in a green coat with narrow bands of gold lace, a scarlet waistcoat trimmed with gold and a small round hat, Baskerville himself was depicted by Dr Alexander Carlyle in about 1760 as 'a great

Albert Place, Ruston Street in the 1950s.

curiosity'. The Scots minister was most struck by the first kitchen at Easy Hill, the fineness of which was a great point in the family and wherein they entertained their company with coffee and chocolate. Baskerville died in 1775 and was buried in his own grounds in a conical structure. In 1821, his home and land were levelled for the making of canal wharves and Baskerville's coffin was found standing upright. The body had not decomposed and the teeth were perfect, but unhappily, for a while his corpse was 'almost made a show of' until a kindly bookseller called Mr Knott placed Baskerville in a vault in Christchurch at the top of New Street. When that church was knocked down at the end of the nineteenth century, Baskerville was re-interred in Warstone Lane cemetery. Today, his genius is brought to mind in front of Baskerville House by a piece of public art which features examples of Baskerville Type.

Bath Row, Attwood Green (formerly Lea Bank)

On his Map of 1731, William Westley drew the site of the Cold Bath and the Ladywell close to where Pershore Street would be cut. Bath Row led to these baths which Hutton described in the late eighteenth century as the most complete in the land. Bathers were charged to use one of seven pools for hot and cold bathing and swimming. Established in 1720, they were sold in the mid 1800s and the place then was used as timber yard.

Ladywell Walk recalls the 'spring of clear, soft and pure water' which provided the water for the baths and which rose to the surface 'and appears in the form of a small enclosed pool of ancient aspect' Named in honour of Our Lady, the Virgin Mary, the wells were mentioned in a document of 1347 which described a 'dwelling in Egebaston Strete leading towards God well feld'. The water from the well was plentiful and helped fill the moat around the manor house (see **Moat Lane**). The ending of the baths led to the covering over of the well and by the late 1800s its waters 'were allowed to flow into the sewers'. They were commemorated by a rusty iron pump. The present location is much more attractive, laid out as it is as the Arcadian.

In later years, Bath Row was marked out by Davenport's Brewery, famed for 'Beer at Home', and the beloved 'Acci', the Accident Hospital. Both these famed Brummie institutions are gone, and today Bath Row and Holloway Head are overlooked by the ruins of Saint Thomas's. Mostly destroyed on 11 December 1940 by enemy bombing in the Second World War, its ruins are fittingly now the Peace Gardens.

Following the regeneration of the Bath Row neighbourhood in the 1950s, it was renamed Lea Bank. Then in the year 2000, the neighbourhood was changed to Attwood Green. Historically the area had not had a name, although it lay on Holloway Head and sometimes was referred to as the Bath Row locality or Upper Edgbaston. Thomas Attwood was a great figure in the history of Birmingham and the United Kingdom. From Halesowen, Attwood came to Birmingham as a young man and joined the bank of Messrs Spooner. Hard working, intelligent and energetic he soon became a partner in the business and at the age of 28 was made high bailiff of Birmingham. The town did not then have a council and local government was split between four bodies: the justices of the peace (magistrates); the Street Commission (see Barker Street); the parish officers who relieved the poor and paid for constables who kept the peace; and the Leet. This was the most ancient of the four groups. It held an annual meeting at which a jury decided on its actions and was responsible for the markets, nuisances and other matters either belonging to the lord of the manor or interfering with his rights.

The Leet had a number of officials who carried out its daily functions. They included a low bailiff who summoned juries to the Leet and charged stallholders at fairs; ale conners who tasted the quality of beers breweed and sold in Birmingham; and flesh conners who ensured that food traders did not sell unwholesome or corupt products. But the most important office was that of the high bailiff who was responsible for the legality of the weights and measures used in the town's markets. Election to high bailiff was an honour and a mark of respect.

Deeply committed to the cause of manufacturers, Attwood was pivotal in the actions against the Orders in Council (see Brougham Street), and in 1829 became the leader of the Birmingham Political Union. This was set up to fight for the reform of

Parliament. At that time, the great majority of electors were wealthy landowners and towns like Birmingham did not even have a Member of Parliament. The BPU fought for the franchise to be extended and for Birmingham and other industrial towns to gain two MPs each. Huge meetings were held in Birmingham, with one of the largest taking place on Newhall Hill on 7 May 1832. The pressure from Birmingham and elsewhere led to the Great Reform Act of 1832 whereby the middle class gained the vote and manufacturing towns were given the right to elect their own MPs.

Unsurprisingly, at the first general election after the act was passed, Attwood was returned unopposed as a member for Birmingham. Because of ill health, he resigned as MP in 1839. His last prominent action in the House of Commons was to present the petition of the Chartists, a working-class movement which was pressing for further reform of Parliament. (See Chartist Road). It was rejected. Although he was 'almost idolised' in Brum, Attwood himself retired into private life and died aged 73 on 6 March 1856 at the Malvern Hills. There is a statue of him in Larches Park, Sparkbrook close to one of his homes at The Larches, hence **Larches Street**, and another at the back of the Town Hall.

Bath Street between Weaman Street and Snow Hill in 1959. Thanks to the *Birmingham Evening Mail*.

Bath Street in the Gun Quarter recalls either the baths which were formerly in **Blews Street** and which became a malthouse about 1820, or a small spring which fed a stream going across Snow Hill to **Water Street**, Hockley and thence into the great pool on the Colmore Estate. **Bath Walk**, Balsall Heath was named after the private swimming baths of John Smith, established in 1846 in **George Street** and condemned and closed down by the local authority in 1878. There is also a **Coldbath Road**, Billesley which takes its name from a stream which runs from Moseley Golf Club, through Moseley Bog and into the River Cole.

Beacon Road, Kingstanding

Like the nearby **Beacon View Drive**, this road relates to Barr Beacon. Recorded as Bearre in 957 and as Barre in the Doomsday Book of 1086, Barr is a Celtic word meaning hill top. At 650 feet above sea level, legends say that Barr Beacon was a sacred place to the Druids, and supposedly in 1588 a great bonfire was prepared there as one in a chain of bonfires across England which would have been lit if the Spanish had invaded at the time of the Armada. Similarly, during the Napoleonic Wars, folk are said to have placed poles, iron, baskets and chains on Barr so as to light a great beacon if French troops had landed. In 1887 it is certain that a huge bonfire celebrated Queen Victoria's diamond jubilee as monarch. It was ventilated by a cross tunnel and chimney and was doused with 26 gallons of oil as well as with tar and creosote.

Outside Birmingham as it is, Barr Beacon was bought in 1918 by Colonel J. H. Wilkinson of Sutton Coldfield. He presented it to the public in memory of the men of the Royal Warwicks and North and South Staffordshire Regiments who had died in the First World War. The dome on its peak was put up in 1933 in memory of Colonel Wilkinson.

Beale Close, Castle Vale

It may be that this close is named after a well-known Birmingham family of the past. A William Beale settled in Birmingham at the end of the eighteenth century, becoming a glass and lead merchant and a follower of Joseph Priestley (see Priestley Road). He and other four other street commissioners were responsible for buying the land on which the Town Hall is built. Beale was followed in the business by his son Samuel, who was a magistrate and one of the first town councillors in Birmingham after incorporation in 1838. Later Samuel became an alderman for Edgbaston, a mayor, a chairman of the Midland Railway, a director of the Birmingham and Midland Bank and MP for Derby 1857-65. He died in 1876. His brother William John Beale was a partner in the legal firm Beale, Marigold and Beale and was a key member of the Orchestral Committee of Musical Festivals which raised money for the General Hospital. He died in 1880. William married Martha Phipson, a member of a family connected to the Rylands (see Ryland Street). Another Beale, Charles Gabriel, was four times lord mayor and became a freeman of the city in 1912.

Bedford Road, Bordesley

According to *Wrightson's Directory* of 1818, a John Bedford of Bordesley was a 'cutler and dealer in sands for various purposes, mourning carriages etc'.

Beales Street, Aston

Edmund Beales was an officer of the Birmingham branch of the Reform League and was active in the campaign which helped bring about the Second Reform Act of 1867, which gave the vote to the skilled of the working-class in towns and cities.

Beech Lanes, Quinton and Warley

This hamlet stretched along that part of the Hagley Road between what is now Balden Road and Lordswood Road. It recalls the rows of beeches which marked the line of the fields between Quinton and Warley. Certainly, there was a Beech Lanes Farm on the south side of the Hagley Road, below Lightwoods Park and just to the east of Fitzroy Avenue. (See Calthorpe Road).

Beeches Road, Perry Barr

The Barr and Aston Local History Society have shown that originally this was called **Brick Kiln Lane** after the brickworks that were located hereabouts. When the area the far side of the Aldridge Road was developed one of the roads was called **Brick Kiln Lane**, although there had been no brick works in this immediate vicinity. Most of the roads on the Beeches Estate recall places in the Peak District such as **Curbar Road**, **Edale Road**, **Hathersage Road** and **Tideswell Road**.

Beilby Road, Stirchley

This was named in 1926 after a surveyor of land.

Bell Street, City

From 1870, the fish market was based in Bell Street. Before that it had been held in Dale End and then from 1851 in the Market Hall, which ran along Bell Street. Bell Street disappeared in the redevelopment of the Bull Ring area in the late 1950s and early 1960s. Joe McKenna believes that Bell Street was cut by Thomas Kempse in 1715 on land leased from William Bell of Alvechurch. However, in 1689 a lease was drawn up between Ambrose Leay and Robert Bell for premises near the 'Crosse' in Birmingham. This was the Market Cross close to the modern Bull Ring and by the spot where Bell Street would be cut sometime before 1731. The document would indicate that Bell Street might be named after Robert Bell. It was in Bell Street that Alfred Bird operated as an experimental chemist. In 1843 he perfected a substitute for yeast in the making of bread and went on to make the first custard powder. His firm grew under his son's direction, and who had built a new factory in Deritend High Street, now the Custard Factory.

The people of Bellbarn Road celebrating VE Day, 5 May 1945, and the end of the war in Europe. Thanks to the *Birmingham Evening Mail*.

Bellbarn Road, Attwood Green (formerly Lea Bank)

According to John Alfred Langford, this road recalls Bell's Barn Ring Farm.

Belliss Street, Edgbaston

Following his apprentice ship to a small engineer in Broad Street, George Edward Belliss took over the firm and advertised himself as a mechanical engineer and boiler maker. In 1863, and still only 26, he began an association with J. S. White of the Isle of Wight. White built service cutters and pinnaces – the small boats belonging to warships – and Belliss made the steam engines that powered them. The machines were light and sturdy and they revolutionised the manufacture of steam launch engines. Belliss did not rest on his laurels. He continually upgraded his machinery, brought in improvements such as an especially high rate of speed, and moved in to the making of steam engines for agricultural and portable uses. In 1872 the business was moved to Ledsam Street, Ladywood, where Belliss was joined in partnership by Alfred Morcom, another clever engineer. Belliss and Morcom's machines were regarded as near to perfection as was possible. Sadly, like so many other great Birmingham manufacturers their history is all that remains. Belliss Street itself was named in 1867.

Bells Lane, Druids Heath

In the later Middle Ages, Hugo de Belne was granted lands in Kings Norton by Edward 1 as a reward for his services as an archer. Some stories go that he was an assassin for the king. He left his name in Bell's Farm, hence Bells Lane, and probably in the enchanting **Bell's Holloway** in Northfield.

Bennetts Hill, City

William Bennett of Birmingham was a cooper and is named in a deed from 1694 relating to his marriage to Joyce, the daughter of James Tayler, a weaver of Tamworth. It might be that Bennetts Hill recalls this man. Certainly in 1698 a Robert Philips of Newton Regis, near Tamworth (see Inge Street) leased out three fields on Bennetts Hill for a term of 120 years to John Hawkesford, a Birmingham bucklemaker. The land included Bennett's Hill, the Banner Cross and Horse Croft, and was let at £18 8s a year. Over time part of the property was surrendered and the Blue Coat School, Saint Philip's and Christchurch (see Christchurch Passage) was built upon it. The rest remained farmland where sheaves of corn swayed in the wind and lads ran up the slopes to pick blackberries. Then, just after the Napoleonic Wars, the lease expired and the fields were cut through with Bennetts Hill itself and **Waterloo Street**, named after the battle at which Napoleon was defeated by the British forces under the Duke of Wellington and the Prussians under Marshall Blucher. (See Blucher Street and Wellington Road).

Eliezer Edwards arrived in Birmingham during the 1830s and stated that architecturally Benetts Hill was the best street of the town. In that decade was born Edward Jones, later Edward Burne-Jones. He grew up in Bennetts Hill, attended King Edward's School, New Street and went on to become a world famous artist. One of the Pre-Raphaelites, Burne-Jones was also a superb craftsman and drew on Arthurian themes and Greek fables for his inspiration. Fittingly, St Philip's Cathedral on Bennetts Hill is graced by two exquisite stained glass windows by Burne-Jones. There is another of his stained glass windows in St Martin's Church in the Bull Ring and some of his paintings are in the Art Gallery.

Benson Road, Winson Green

Descended from a Yorkshire family, Edward White Benson was born in Birmingham in 1829. His father was a well known manufacturing chemist and he himself attended King Edward's School, New Street, going from there to Trinity College, Cambridge. After a distinguished teaching career he focused upon religious life, becoming the first Bishop of Truro in 1877. Six years later he was anointed the Archbishop of Canterbury, retaining this office until he died in 1896. His time as archbishop was noted for its activity, especially with regard to relations with Christians in the Middle East. In the 1802 Enclosure Award for Birmingham Heath (see Heath Street) the line of Benson Road and part of Factory Road was known as **Ninevah Lower Road** (see Ninevah Road).

Benson Road, Winson Green in the late nineteenth century.

Berrowside Road

The North Arden and Shard End Local History Societies note the Iron Age berrow or barrow at the rear of this road, where some ancient tools have been found.

Betholom Row, Five Ways

This narrow and short passage off Islington Row has all but disappeared, but it was the site of the Jewish cemetery from 1823 until the 1870s. Vivian Bird states that in Hebrew, Beth Olom means the City of the Dead. There is another Jewish cemetery called Beth Olom in Brooklyn, New York.

Billesley Lane, Moseley

Originally Bully or Bulleys Lane, Billesley Lane now takes its name from the district which means the clearing in the wood made by Bill.

Birchall Street, Deritend

In 1890, Joseph Hill drew a conjectural plan of Birmingham in 1553. As his sources, he used private surveys, old plans and the surveys of Birmingham carried out in the reigns of Henry VIII and Queen Mary. On his plan, he placed enclosures called the Great and Little Buckstalls and also the Birchills Pasture. Toulmin Smith believed that this pasture had belonged to the lord of Birmingham and was planted with birch

Billesley Lane Moseley.

Photo. Sam. G. Mason

Billesley Lane, Moseley at the end of the nineteenth century.

trees, hence Byrcheill. In Westley's Map of 1731, Birchall Street was called **Brick Kiln Lane** and in Hanson's Map of 1778 it was given as **Birch Hole Street**. Buckstalls were means to trap wild or stray dear and were illegal except for persons who possessed a deer park, chase or forest – and the area which is now the top end of Bradford Street once was a deer park. Another explanation for the name Birchall is that it relates to a landowner, although I believe this less likely. Like Bradford Street and Lombard Street, Birchall Street was the scene of activity by one of the world's earliest building societies in 1781 (see also Bradford Street and Cheapside).

Birches Green Road, Erdington

The Birch family lived locally in the sixteenth century and gave their name to Birches Green Farm which was overlaid with council housing during the inter-war years.

Birchfield Road, Birchfield

The Birchfield Road runs through a district which once was one of the hamlets of Handsworth. It is likely that it takes its name not from a family called Birch but from the birch trees which were noticeable in its fields. The district was developed from

Preparing for the underpass on the Birchfield Road in 1962. This photo is taken from the junction with Mansfield Road. Thanks to the *Birmingham Evening Mail*.

the nineteenth century and had its own parish church, Holy Trinity – hence **Trinity Road**. Designed by J. A. Chatwin in the Early English style, it was consecrated in 1864. To the north of Trinity Road, the neighbourhood is filled with roads named after other parts of England, especially Kent – as in **Canterbury Road** – and the west country, as in **Tewkesbury Road.**

Bissell Close, Hall Green

Coming off Gresham Road, this is named after John Bissell. In his will he made allowance to pay monies to the schoolmaster of Hall Green to buy a coat for a poor man in the Swanshurst Quarter (see Swanshurst Lane) of Yardley Parish. The coat was to be marked JB on the left sleeve. **Bissell Street**, Highgate, emerged in the mid 1800s and was cut out of Bissell's Meadows. **Bissell Street**, Quinton, close to the High Street and the Hagley Road, harks back to James Bissell, a property owner locally. His successors developed his land for building in the late nineteenth century.

Blake Lane, Small Heath and Little Bromwich

Blake Lane indicated the boundary between the old manors of Bordesley and Little Bromwich. Bob Marsden, an expert of Small Heath, explains that at 435 feet above sea level the spot is the highest point in the area and was on the edge of Hob Moor (see Hobmoor Road). As such it was windswept and bleak – hence Blake Street. It should be remembered that in the West Midlands dialect, the 'ea' vowel sound is prounced as 'ay', hence Bleak would be spoken as Blake. Joe McKenna disagrees, feeling that Blake is derived from the blackness of the soil or from a man called Blaca. The nearby **Blakelands Street** is obviously connected with Blake Lane.

Blews Street, Aston

Now with an Aston post code, Blews Street was always within the manor of Birmingham given that it was south of the boundary of the Aston Brook. Two men with the name of Blews stand out in the history of Brum. They are William Blews, a maltster in Pinfold Street, who is mentioned in *Wrightson's Directory* of 1818; and H.M. Blews who restored the ancient monuments of the lords of Birmingham in Saint Martin's in the Bull Ring in 1846. Given that Blews Street was one of the streets cut out in the New Town which developed in the late 1700s and early 1800s to the east of Newtown Row, then Blews Street cannot be named after H. M. Blews.

Bloomsbury Street, Duddeston

Like **Fleet Street**, **Ludgate Hill** and others, Bloomsbury Street was so called after its London counterpart.

Blucher Street, Attwood Gardens (formerly Lea Bank)

Marshall Gebherd Lebercht von Blucher led the Prussian forces which were crucial in the Duke of Wellinngton's victory over Napoleon at the Battle of Waterloo in 1815. He is also recalled in the nearby **Marshall Street**. Born in 1742, he went into the Swedish Army when he was fourteen, later joining the Prussian Army after he was captured in battle. A heavy drinker and womaniser, Blucher was an aggressive and brave leader who became know as Marshall Forward for his trait of pushing onwards. After a controversial career, which included his retirement and re-entry into the Prussian Army, he was reponsible for the defeat of Napoleon at the Battle of Leipzig in 1814 and for the subsequent capture of Paris. Overcome, Napoleon abdicated and was exiled to the small island of Elba, returning from there to France soon after. Now aged 72, Blucher once again came out of retirement to play a vital role in Napoleon's final defeat at Waterloo. He died four years later.

Rowland Hill, the originator of our present postal system, was born in Kidderminster in 1795 but came to Birmingham with his parents when he was aged seven. His father ran a school on the corner of Blucher Street, later moving it to Hazelwood on the Hagley Road and opposite Portland Road. When Hill tried to get his postal proposals off the ground he was cursed 'as a fellow from Birmingham coming to teach people their business'. Finally, in 1839 he succeeded and a new postage law introduced an experimental rate of 4d per letter. This was soon reduced to a 1d postage for a letter weighing half an ounce. Rowland Hill's brother, Matthew Davenport Hill, later became became recorder of Birmingham and played a major role in the legal life of the town.

Marshall Street is on the left in this photo from the late 1950s, and it looks like it is taken from Upper Gough Street.

Today Blucher Street is best known for the beautiful Singers Hill Synagogue. Opened in 1856, it replaced a place of worship in Severn Street that had been dedicated in 1809. By the later nineteenth century, Singers Hill Synagogue was at the heart of one of Birmingham's two small Jewish quarters. (See Ellis Street and Inge Street). It remains a focus of Orthodox Jewish worship.

Boden Road, Hall Green

Norman A. Worwood has written as an exaptriate Brummie to state that the story of this name comes from 'an unimpeachable source, one Geoffrey Boden (now deceased), a colleague of mine who rose through the ranks of Birmingham Municipal Bank to become its Superintendent of Branches, from which post he retired in 1974 at the age of 65'. He recounted that his only daughter, Angela, left school and went to work in department of the Council responsible for naming roads. The senior officers were casting around for a new name, spotted the new junior clerk who was called Miss Boden and decided it was just right for Boden Road, Hall Green.

Boldmere Road, Sutton Coldfield

Probably derived from Baldmoor which was pronounced locally as Bolmer, Joe McKenna feels that it means the house (bold) near a lake (mere) or a moor.

Booth's Lane, Great Barr

William Booth was a notorious forger and minter of false coins and on 28 March 1812, the military attacked his fortified farmhouse in Great Barr, hence **Booth's Farm Road**. When he was captured the authorities found £3,000 in good notes, 200 guineas in gold, £600 in counterfeit silver coins and a large amount forged notes. He was sent for trial at Stratford Assizes. Four years previously he had been tried at Warwick for the murder of his brother, John, but had been acquitted for lack of evidence. This time he was not so fortunate. Booth was executed publicly on 15 August 1815, but the hangman bungled the job and so the coiner had to be revived and hanged again two hours later. He was buried at Handsworth Old Church and later moved. Thus, Booth was tried twice, hanged twice and buried twice.

From the seventeenth century at least, Birmingham's fashioners of metal were gaining a high reputation for inventiveness and quality. However, that ingenuity led some to use their talents negatively in the making of base coins. This encouraged some influential people to regard Birmingham with disdain and to the name Brummagem becoming synonomous with base or counterfeit ware. This bad name was made worse by writers such as the poet John Dryden, who as a staunch Royalist hated Birmingham for having been a place of keen Parliamentarian support in the English Civil War. It was Dryden who penned the lines in 1682, ''Twas coined by stealth, like groats in Birmingham'. The infamy of Brummagem coins and the need to improve perceptions of the town's wares, motivated Matthew Boulton in the later eighteenth century to begin the minting of coins. This imperative also encouraged him and others to use the name Birmingham instead of Brummagem (see Boulton Road). Over the next few decades, false coining declined markedly – and no doubt, the execution of Booth played a part in that decline.

Bordesley Green Road, Bordesley Green

Named after the district alongside which it runs, it brings to mind 'La Grene de Bordeslie', reference to which Bob Marsden has found in the thirteenth century. In those days it was an area of common pasture on the borders of Saltley and Bordesley Manors. Bordesley Green Road itself emerged in the later nineteenth century.

Bordesley High Street

Referring both to a district and a road running from Camp Hill to High Street, Deritend, the name Bordesley means the clearing in the wood of a man called Bord or else the clearing where boards were available. Named just as Bordesley, Bordesley High Street was amongst the streets included in the *Survey of the Borough of Birmingham* in 1553. Unlike, the development of High Street, Deritend, that of High Street, Bordesley was slow but by the 1860s it had become filled in with shops and small factories and from 1899 it was dominated by the Bordesley Palace on the corner of Bordesley High Street and Clyde Street. In the early twentieth century, Bordesley High Street was distnictive for its raised footpath, below which ran the road. This indicated that it was one of the holloways of Birmingham, whereby the road itself was hollowed out by centuries of passage of feet and hooves (see Holloway Head). The road was also well known for the sweet shop of the famed boxer Joe Fox, in the front window of which was hung his Lonsdale Belt.

Other street names associated with Bordesley include **Bordesley Park Road**, which follows the line of the boundary of the park of Bordesley Hall. This was the home of John Taylor, the famed Brummagem button king of the eighteenth century who was a co-founder of Taylor and Lloyd's Bank. According to Hutton, our first historian, this producer of buttons was 'the Shakespeare or Newton of his day' and his achievements were essential in the riches, extension and improvement of Birmingham. Little is known about Taylor's early life, although he was born about 1711 and it is thought that he worked for a time as a cabinet maker. What is certain is that he made his fortune as a gilder of metal buttons – a process whereby the goods were covered with a thin layer of gold leaf or were plated in a similar way with silver.

By the mid-eighteenth century, Taylor was employing 500 workers in a factory which impressed Lord Shelbourne, a leading politician, and other dignitaries. In his *Life of Johnson*, Boswell proclaimed that Taylor was one 'who by his ingenuity in mechanical inventions, and his success in the trade, gained an immense fortune'. (See Doctor Johnson Passage). Taylor's descendants continued to be prominent in Birmingham and were associated with Moseley Hall. Bordesley Hall itself was

Bordesley Park Road in the 1930s. Thanks to the *Birmingham Evening Mail*.

enclosed by 30 acres of park land, which boasted an ornamental lake and in which deer roamed. This estate was built upon in the 1850s. **Bordesley Street** was described as a new street in the late 1780s and was intended 'to be carried for a mile all the way to Bordesley from Park Street'. It never reached Bordesley, ending at Little Anne Street just before the River Rea.

Botetourt Road, Weoley Castle

At the time of the Domesday Book in 1086, one of the greatest Norman magnates in England was William FitzAnsculf. He held wide lands throughout the south of England and in the West Midlands, where he was the baron of Dudley. Through this barony he was overlord of the manors of Aston, Birmingham, Edgbaston, Erdington, Handsworth, Little Barr, Perry and Witton. His successors also controlled a number of manors which are mentioned first in the twelfth or thirteenth centuries, such as Bordesley, Duddeston, Little Bromwich, Nechells and Saltley. After FitzAnsculf's death, his possessions went to Gervaise Paganel, thus **Paganel Road**, California. Paganel died without an heir and his lands passed through his sister, Hawise, to her husband Roger de Somery, hence **Somery Road**, California.

In 1322, John de Somery died with no male heir and his properties were passed to the families of his sisters. The youngest, Joan, was the widow of Thomas Botetourt, the son of John de Botetourt, a distinguished soldier and Admiral of the Fleet in in 1294. Thomas died before his father and so Joan gained the manors of Handsworth and Edgbaston, and the family's lands in Aston and Weoley. She lived at Weoley Castle, a fortified manor house. In 1424 it was described as 'the Castell with a water called the mote compassing the 1st castell, in which is a great halle with a great chambre in the upper ende'. Later known as Weoley Castle, this moated manor house had six turrets of stone and was in the midst of a large park containing deer pools filled with fish. Joan was a fiery person and on one occasion was involved in besieging her sister who held Dudley Castle. Her son, John, was a soldier of repute in the French Wars. He died in 1385 and was succeeded by his grand-daughter, Joyce, who was married to Hugh Burnell, Lord Burnell, who is recalled in **Burnel Road**, California.

Boulton Road, Handsworth

Running down from the Soho Road towards the Hockley Brook and the Handsworth New Road and cut out in 1843, Boulton Road was named after the most celebrated of Brummie manufacturers. In the words of Samuel Timmins, 'among the industrial heroes of the world and the greatest men of Birmingham, Matthew Boulton will ever hold the loftiest place'. Born in 1728, whilst yet just seventeen Boulton invented the means of inlaying buttons, buckles and trinkets, or toys as such small metal goods were known. By his late twenties he was running his father's toy manufactory in Snow Hill, but so successful did he become that he found his expansion was hindered by the smallness of his premises. Consequently, he took on the lease of land at Soho, just across the Hockley Brook and in the separate parish of Handsworth, Staffordshire. It was a good choice, for the buildings were large, there was a mill for slitting metal, and there was a large pool – the water from which could power larger machinery. Moreover, the Soho Works was close to the Wolverhampton Road (now the Soho Road) down which came coal from Wednesbury.

Helped by his wife's money, Boulton built a magnificent new works in 1764-5, recalled today by **Factory Road**, Handsworth. It cost the huge sum of £10,000 and was an expensive investment. Boulton's costs were increased by his determination to pay the highest wages to attract the best and most artistic craftsmen and designers. If money was tight, so too was water and in seeking an alternative source of power, in 1774 Boulton went into partnership with the Scot, James Watt, to develop an efficient steam engine. Later made at the Soho Foundry in Smethwick, hence **Foundry Road**, Winson Green, the steam engines of Boulton and Watt helped to thrust Britain into industrial supremacy. A wonderful inventor, Watt appreciated the varied talents of Boulton. Not only was the Brummie industrialist 'an ingenious mechanick, well skilled in all the practices of the Birmingham manufacaturers but possessed in a high degree the faculty of rendering any new invention of his own or others useful to the publick by organizing & arranging the processes by which it could be carried on, as well as of promoting the sale by his own exertions & by his numerous friends & correspondents . . . When he took any scheme in hand he was rapid in executing it . . . He was a liberal encourager of merit in others & to him rthe country is indebted for various improvements . . . '

Matthew Boulton was a leading figure in the renowned Lunar Society, that group of manufacturers, thinkers and scientists which made such an impact upon the history of the world, and he is one of the most important figures in the history of Birmingham. He strove against the belief that was held by many people that Brummagem ware was base or counterfeit. This he did through making sure that his products were designed to the best standards, were made with the finest materials and were crafted by the most cunning of workers. In a further attempt to promote the good name of Birmingham he was instrumental in the successful campaign for the town to have its own Assay Office, where the local gold and silver ware could be tested and stamped for their worthiness. Boulton was also active in the ensuring that a canal was cut between Birmingham and the Black Country, as a result of which coal could be brought in more swiftly and cheaply. He died in 1809 and his funeral was attended by thousands of Brummies who recognised his greatness.

Boulton lived at Soho House, which now is open to the public. His son, Matthew Robinson Boulton, bought the Tew Park Estate in Gloucestershire and after his death, the properties in Handsworth and Birmingham were developed following an Act of Parliament in 1874. This urbanisation led to the emergence of **Tew Park Road** which cuts across from Boulton Road to Ninevah Road.

Bournbrook Road, Bournbrook

Rising in Quinton, the Bournbrook runs along the northern boundary of the district of Bournbrook, separating it from Edgbaston. The early English used the word burna (bourne) for a stream which was large and which had gravel beds and clear water with submerged plants. Thus Bournbrook means the brook brook.

Bournville Lane, Bournville

Before the Cadbury family started their chocolate factory locally in 1879, this district was a greenfield site in King's Norton and Northfield, Worcsetershire. The name Bournville was chosen for the new works because of the Bourn Brook which ran through the locality and because 'ville' suggested a French town – and French chocolate was regarded as the best in those days. The Cadbury factory faced on to a lane which became known as Bournville Lane. Most of the other streets locally raise up woodland scenes, for example with **Elm Road**, **Sycamore Road** and **Willow Road**.

Looking down Bournville Lane, Stirchley from Lea House Road and towards Hazelwell Street, later the Pershore Road.

Bowcroft Grove, Sutton Coldfield

This marks the site of a field close to Pype Hayes Park and Hall where it is told two bow-bearers had a lodge. Their duty was to take care of travellers crossing the dangerous common between the Chester Road and Sutton Coldfield.

Bracebridge Road, Sutton Coldfield

The Bracebridge family was one of the oldest in Warwickshire and like the Ardens was also descended from Turchill de Arden, in the Bracebridge's case through his second wife, Leveruna. It was through her that the manor of Kingsbury descended to the Bracebridges. In 1419, the Earl of Warwick granted Sutton Manor House, its park and pools to Sir Ralph Bracebridge in his lifetime. In return Bracebridge sent nine lancers and seventeen bowmen to the English garrison in Calais. Soon after the grant, Sir Ralph made Bracebridge Pool in Sutton Park, so that he might have a supply of bream for his household. (See also Arden Road. For **Bracebridge Street**, Aston see Holte Road and for **Bracebridge Road**, Erdington see Pype Hayes Road).

Bradford Road, Castle Bromwich

For centuries, the manor of Castle Bromwich was held by the Devereux family, but in 1657 Anne Devereux sold her lands locally to the Bridgemans, who later became the Earls of Bradford. The family did take some interest in the affairs of nearby

Birmingham and Sir Henry Bridgeman was one of the first committee members of the General Hospital. Sir Henry was created Baron Bradford in 1794, hence **Bradford Road**, Castle Bromwich.

Bradford Street, Deritend

Seeking to kick start the development of his estate in Deritend, in 1767 Henry Bradford offered the freehold to the first person to build a house upon his land – through which ran the aptly-named Bradford Street. This move was encouraged by the opening that year of the turnpike road to Alcester. (See **Alcester Road**). Four years later, land for building leases in Bradford Street was advertised at three farthings the square yard. Although a building society was active here from 1781 (see also Cheapside), progress was slow and in 1805 mention was made of the removal of the hill at the top of Bradford Street, from which the soil was carried to the lower parts.

Bradford himself was a prominent Quaker and dealer in timber and it was to him that George Fentham had devised the Warner Fields Estate out of which Bradford Street and **Warner Street** were formed. This estate is indicated in the archives of King Edward's School in a document from 1511, when Lord de Ferrers held 'divers crofts of pasture called Warner's Fields, late William Cowper's and before that John Le Warner's'. It is likely that John le Warner had gained his name because his ancestors had been warreners locally, looking after land where game was bred.

Brandwood Road, Brandwood End

Both the road and the area are probably derived from the Middle English word brend, meaning burnt. In 1519 a William Roper was mentioned as living at Brande Ende. In the Enclosure Awards for the Manor of Kings Norton in 1774, the road is given as **Branderd Road**.

Brasshouse Passage, City

During the nineteenth century it was stated that 'as Manchester is to cotton, Bradford is to wool and Sheffield is in steel, then Birmingham is in brass'. The brass trade had emerged in the late 1700s when the local brassfounders were described as 'ingenious artists who make an infinite variety of articles'. To cater for their demand for brass, a brasshouse was set up in Broad Street in 1781, recalled now in Brasshouse Passage.

Brays Road, Sheldon

Thomas Bray was the rector of Sheldon and in 1696 he was assigned to help the youthful church in Maryland in the United States of America. To help him in his task, Bray started the Society for the Propogation of Christian Knowledge. In 1922 the Bishop of Birmingham was presented with the state flag of Maryland in recognition of Bray's achievements. It hangs in St Philips Cathedral.

Bread Street

Birmingham boasted two streets of this strange name in the nineteenth century. The first became Cornwall Street in 1898 (see Colmore Row); and the second was off Hill Street. Like its namesake, this street was cut in the eighteenth century. It was cleared in 1882.

Brearley Street, Handsworth

The Brearleys were a well established Handsworth family. In the parish church of Saint Mary there are memorials to Anna Maria Sacherevall of New Hall, Warwickshire and Jane Gough of Perry Hall (see Gough Road), the co-heiresses of William Brearley. A monument outside the church commemorates Martha, the wife of Joseph Brearley, who died in 1804. Brearley Street runs between Crockets Lane and Brewery Street.

Breedon Road, Cotteridge

The Tithe Map of 1840-1 indicates a Breedon House owned by a John Lane Snow. It is now the site of Cotteridge Primary Schools. There was also a Breedon Cross Farm locally which was farmed by the Cheshires in the 1870s. Bre is a Celtic word meaning hill, whilst don is an Anglo-Saxon word also signifying hill. It may be that the name is taken from that of Breedon on the Hill in Worcestershire and it seems likely that the early Anglo-Saxon settlers of this neighbourhood heard the British folk talking of the 'bre' and thought that this was the name of the hill. Thus Breedon Hill actually contains the word hill three times.

Brick Kiln Lane, City

This short street ran off Lancaster Street (formerly Walmer Lane). Cut by the 1780s, it indicates the presence of brick works – a common feature in an expanding town. These works were noted in an advertisement in the early nineteenth century which indicated the sale of 120,000 bricks as well as land of clay and sand with soft water at Walmer Lane. **Brickfield Road**, Hay Mills and **Kiln Lane** running off it take their name from the Waterloo Brick Works, hence **Waterloo Road**, South Yardley.

Bridge Street, City

Named because it went over the Birmingham to Worcester Canal, Bridge Street was first shown on Hanson's map of 1781. On Hanson's map of 1795, **Wharf Street** is shown running from it, so called after the large canal wharf which lay behind it. In the mid-nineteenth century, Bridge Street was best known as the location of the cocoa and chocolate factory of the Cadbury family. **Bridge Road**, Saltley goes over the London and Birmingham Railway, one of Birmingham's first two railways that was opened in 1838 and which originally terminated at Curzon Street. Finally, the tiny **Bridge Road**, Sparkhill, off Percy Road, goes towards the River Cole and the Greet Bridge over it.

Brindley Place, City

James Brindley was the great canal engineer in charge of the cutting of the Birmingham Canal. Opened in 1772 it went from Paradise Wharf to Auderley near Wolverhampton and linked Birmingham with the Black Country coal and iron fields. The new quicker means of transportation resulted in a dramatic fall in the cost of these essential raw materials. At Auderley the canal joined with the Grand Trunk system of waterways, so that in effect Birmingham was connected to the great ports of Liverpool and Bristol. Because this last town lay on the Severn it led to the naming of **Severn Street** (originally **Cross Street**) close to the offices of the Birmingham Canal Navigations, hence **Navigation Street**. Having a brilliant mind, Brindley was unable to read and write and solved most of his problems without writings of drawings. **Brunel Street** comemmorates another famous engineer, Isambard Kingdom Brunel. Amongst many notable projects, he designed the 'Great Eastern' (1853) steamship. The largest vessel built till that time, it was raised from its dry dock on to the Thames by hydraulic machinery from Tangye's of Smethwick.

There was also a **Canal Street** off Lancaster Street, named after the nearby Birmingham to Fazeley Canal – for which an act of Parliament was gained in 1783. **New Canal Street** and **Fazeley Street** came about after the Digbeth Branch of this canal was opened in 1790. The Birmingham to Fazeley Canal provided a connection with London via the Coventry, Oxford and Grand Junction Canals, hence **Oxford Street**, and also with Liverpool, thus **Liverpool Street**. In Erdington **Canal Lane** also relates to the Birmingham and Fazeley Canal. **Wharf Lane** and **Wharf Street**, Hockley are across Park Road from the Soho Pool Wharf; **Wharf Road** and **Wharfdale Road**, Tyseley lead to a wharf on the Birmingham to Warwick Canal; and **Wharf Street**, Aston, off Wainwright Street, was close to the Birmingham and Fazeley Canal. In Kings Norton, **Wharf Road** is the continuation of Parsons Hill and is named after a wharf on the Worcester to Birmingham Canal, which also gives rise to **Canal Side**.

Bristol Road, Edgbaston, Bournbrook, Selly Oak, Northfield and Longbridge

In the later Middle Ages, the road from Worcester to Tyneside was described as one of the great royal roads. It passed through Droitwich, Bromsgrove and Birmingham before going on to Lichfield and thence to the north east. Henry III passed along this way in 1237 when Letters Close were dated at Birmingham, and in 1486 Henry VII also came through Birmingham on his way from Nottingham to Worcester. The road was turnpiked in 1726, becoming the property of a private company which was authorised by act of Parliament to charge tolls on travellers and to maintain the road. In 1853, the Public Works Committee of the Town Council furnished parts of it with kerbstones and sewers and in 1872 it was taken over by the corporation.

Twelve years previously, the Bristol Road Trees Committee had been formed with the objective of planting trees along the road. Under the leadership of Councillor Robert Pollock, a steel tool maker, it was so successful that its example was taken up by the council in 1875. This was during Joseph Chamberlain's mayoralty and the first action by the corporation was to plant plane trees, limes and poplars in Stephenson Place. The *Birmingham Daily Post* reported on 30 November 1870 that 'some forty or fifty curious passers-by witnessed the proceedings, and thus unconsciously assisted the commencement of a new aesthetic era in municipal matters'. The next year 100 planes were planted on Broad Street, supposedly because Chamberlain could not abear the naked sight of Broad Street as he rode in his carriage from his home in Edgbaston to the Council House.

Other roads connecting to this route have names of places to the south west of Birmingham: **Worcester Street** was obvious by the early 1700s and ran into **Smallbrook Street**; originally known as **Bath Road, Bristol Street** was the road to Bromsgrove and Worcester and was apparent from the end of the eighteenth century; **Exeter Row**, which was the bottom end of Holloway Head, was noted in advertisement for building land in 1764; and **Bromsgrove Street** emerged in the 1780s. Writing in 1866 a correspondent to the *Daily Gazette* recalled that at the end of the eighteenth century there 'was nothing but beautiful and fertile gardens' at the back of Bromsgrove Street, and 'many a time I have wandered through them, along the "Pudding Brook" walk' (see Claybrook Street).

Bristol Street in 1952.

Brittle Street, City

Obvious by the first years of the nineteenth century, Brittle Street went between Livery Street and Snow Hill. It is named after a local family and in 1766 a lease for land in Snow Hill was made between Isaac and Nathaniel Whitehead Benjamin and Benjamin Brettel. The street was cleared for the building of Snow Hill Station in1852.

Broad Street, City

That part of Dale End between Carrs Lane and Bull Street and Lower Priory was originally called Broad Street, the name dropping out of use by Bradford's Map of 1750. At that date, the modern Broad Street was a merely a country path which led from **Bewdley Street** (now Victoria Square) and **Swinford Street** (the top end of New Street) to Five Ways and hence to Stourbridge and Bewdley. By the 1780s, the path in that locality had been widened because of the home at Easy Hill of the celebrated printer, John Baskerville. (See Easy Row). The rest of the route was broadened soon after. This was because of the emergence of the Islington Estate on

This is beautiful photo taken by an A. Marshall who lived at 2 back of 216 Conybere Street and who called the shot, 'Autumn Sunshine in Broad Street'. The boys are standing outside the 'Prince of Wales' theatre, destroyed by bombing in the Second World War.

land owned by Saint Martin's Church between **Islington Row** and the top end of Broad Street, or as it was termed until 1874, **Islington**.

The development of this glebe land was allowed by an act of Parliament passed in 1773 and within fifteen years building had begun. (See Glebe Farm). Amongst the streets which were laid out were the well-named **Saint Martin's Street** and the equally religious sounding **Bishopsgate Street**. In the nineteenth century the short **Glebe Street** (originally **Hanover Street**) was cut across the other side of Broad Street. It recalled the land ownership of Saint Martin's and was cleared in the 1930s after its houses were declared as slums.

Bromford Lane, Erdington, Bromford and Ward End

In 1656 the lane was called **Clayhole Lane** and in the Enclosure Awards for the Manors of Erdington and Witton in 1804, it was named **Green Man Road** after the 'Old Green Man' inn, now 'The Lad in the Lane'. This is claimed to be the oldest pub in Warwickshire. The name Bromford itself is also an old one. Bromford Mill was on the north bank of the Tame and fell within the manor of Erdington and probably it was the mill mentioned for that area in the Doomsday Book of 1086. Certainly a Bromford mill is noted in the early twelfth century. In 1285 a 'stagnum de Bramford' was recorded and within a hundred years, Bromford Bridge was also named. Before the First World War, Bromford Lane was remembered as very narrow and darkened by trees which grew on high banks and the branches of which overlapped with each other. The district of Bromford, featuring **Bromford Drive** and **Bromford Road**, belonged originally to Castle Bromwich and was brought to national attention by the Birmingham racecourse here. When this was developed as a housing estate many of its road names were taken from other racecourses, hence **Kempson Road**, **Doncaster Way** and **Towcester Croft**, or from celebrated racehorses, as with **Hyperion Road** and **Arkle Croft**.

Bromsgrove Street

Linking the Bull Ring with Bristol Street and hence Bromsgrove, this street appears on Hanson's Map of 1785.

Brook Road, Edgbaston

According to Sparrey's plan of Edgbaston in 1718, what is now the bottom of Brook Road and Westfield Road, Edgbaston was called **Snailes Green**.

Brookfields Road, Brookfields

For hundreds of years the western part of Birmingham, beyond Icknield Street, was known as Birmingham Heath. A great expanse of shrubland it included a couple of more fertile spots such as Winson Green (see also Winson Green Road) and Brookfields – through the fields of which a brook did run. Owned by the Gooch familiy (see Gooch Street), Brookfields was developed slowly over thirty years from the 1830s. Brookfields Road is at the westernmost edge of Brookfields, running from Crabtree Road to the old City Fever Hospital.

Brookvale Park Road and Brookvale Road, Witton

The pool in Brookvale Park was originally called Lower Witton Reservoir and supplied water to Birmingham. In the late nineteenth century it was renamed Brookvale, after the nearby Brook Farm (also Faulkener's Farm) and **Brook Vale** on the lower end of Gipsy Lane. Brookvale Road itself was formerly named **Witton Lane**.

Broom Hall Crescent, Acocks Green

Broom Hall Farm was mentioned as early as 972 when it was given as Bromhalas, meaning the nook or corner of land where broom grew. In the later Middle Ages, the estate was owned by the de Bromhales, a family like many others which took its name from the spot where they lived and which lived in a moated manor. The family died out in the fifteenth century and their lands were split up. However, the name of Broomhall continued to be given to half of Yardley Parish – although in succeeding centuries the area covered by Broomhall shrank drastically. By the early nineteenth century, Broomhall Farm was owned by the Kings. Its last tenants were Joseph Wheldon Izod and his wife, Fanny Sophia King. They farmed there between about 1921-47 and had moved there from Hall Green Farm. Parts of Broom Hall Farm were sold from 1929, with the final sections disappearing in 1947.

Brougham Street, Lozells

This was one of the first streets laid out in Lozells and was cut by 1839. It was named after Lord Brougham who was on 'very intimate terms of friendship' with James Watt junior who lived at Aston Hall. Brougham was a frequent visitor and according to Eliezer Edwards, the favourite seat of the two was in a temple-like summer house near to Quilter's pool in the large grounds of the hall. As Lord Chancellor, Lord Brougham was a great reformer of the courts, but for Brummies he was better known as a man who championed the cause of manufacturers in Parliament during the Napoleonic Wars when the Orders in Council forbade trade with the continent. These caused great problems for many of Birmingham's trades which depended upon exports for their well being and when they were revoked in 1812 there was great rejoicing. The then Mr Brougham was especially signalled out for thanks for his efforts and he was presented with two richly embossed tureens made at the Soho Works. They were inscribed to 'Henry Brougham Esq., the enlightened Advocate of the manufacturing and commercial Interests of his country . . .'

Browning Street, Ladywood

Changed from **Tindal Street** in 1894, this street brings to mind the poet Robert Browning, who died five years before the change of name. Married to Elizabeth Barrett, a famous female poet, Browning is best known for *Men and Women* (1855) and *Dramatis Personae* (1864). The couple lived in Florence from 1846.

Browns Green, Handsworth

Originally Medieval pastureland by the junction of the modern Handsworth Wood Road and Hamstead, Browns Green relates to a Roger Browne who paid 4s 10d for the rental of a field hereabouts in 1538.

Brownsea Drive, Attwood Green

This is best known as the site of the headquarters of the Girl Guides in Birmingham and Margery Elliott informs me that this road is named after Brownsea Island in Poole Harbour, Dorset. Originally, the Girl Guides used to meet in the old Hebrew Schools in Blucher Street. This building had been purchased when the Jewish School moved to Saint Lukes Road and Margery believes the Cadburys were involved in the purchase as Mrs W. A. Cadbury was County Commissioner of the Girl Guides. When the Inner Ring Road was planned, the City told the Girl Guides that their building would be demolished and rebuilt in a new, short street. The Girl Guides wanted this called Trefoil Street, but the Council refused as the name existed elsewhere in the city. Accordingly, Brownsea was chosen as it it was where Baden-Powell held his first experimental boys' camp in 1907 – from which arose the scouting movement. The new building, Trefoil House, was opened by Princess Margaret when Margery's sister was County Secretary.

Buck Street

Obvious by Bradford's Plan of Birmingham of 1750, this short street was thrust from history by the building of Aston University. It is associated with the nearby Doe Street and appears to be a play upon the names for male and female deers.

Buckland End Lane, Buckland End

Originally known as Bockenholt, the beech (bocken) wood (holt), Bucklands End was in Castle Bromwich until 1931 and was developed with Shard End. Bucklands End Lane formerly was the wonderfully-named **Maggoty Lane**, whilst **Buckland End** and part of the **Heath Way** was called **Black Mire Lane**. A deed from the thirteenth century states that William, son of John the Cuper of Bokenholt, granted to Henry of Yardley a piece of land in Bokenholt

A wonderful view of the old Bull Ring in the 1950s. It was taken by Michael F Cann. Known as Mike, he began his working life in the stage lighting department of the Birmingham Theatre in the mid 40s. He joined the *Birmingham Despatch* as a trainee staff photographer in the late 40s and started as a freelance photographer in the late 50s when the *Despatch* closed. Mike then worked on the Birmingham Post and Mail, joining the *Birmingham Planet* in 1963 as chief photographer, where he was responsible for producing all the pictures in the first dummy edition. Mike returned to freelance work when the *Planet* ceased publication in 1967 and joined the PR department at IMI, Witton, continuing to work for them as staff and freelance photographer until his death in 2001. Thanks to the family of Mike Cann.

Bull Ring, City

Properly, the Bull Ring was that stretch of road which ran between Moor Street and Park Street. It is first recorded as 'leBullrynge' in the Charter of King Edward's School in 1552, and according to William Hawkes Smith writing in 1825, its name 'arose from certain priveliges granted to one John Cooper, who flourishing in the High Street, about three hundred years ago, and who was a benefactor to the town. One of the remunerating priveliges claimed by the said Cooper was 'that he should bait a bull in this part of the town whenever he pleased.' Until the redvelopment of the area in the 1960s, a bull ring was attached to a wall in the Bull Ring.

The Bull Ring was not named on Westley's Map of 1731 nor on *Bradford's Map* of 1751. Instead its course was called **Corn Cheaping** (see also Cheapside). However, in 1757 the **Great Bull Ring** is mentioned in an advertisement and the Bull Ring itself is indicated on Hanson's map of 1781. In 1806 the Street Commissioners of Birmingham, then the local authority, cleared the houses on the eastern side of Spiceal Street and on the western side of the Bull Ring and lower High Street. This opened up a great triangle of space which had Saint Martin's at its base and which became the Bull Ring of memory. All the market traders were gathered here and the whole area became known as the Bull Ring.

In 1825 William Hawkes Smith evoked the thrilling atmosphere on Mondays, Thursdays and Saturdays, the market days. He declared that especially on a Saturday evening 'there are few more bustling or more cheerfully noisy scenes than that presented by the Birmingham market place'. The innumerable lights gave the area 'the brilliancy of a well-illuminated room. The show of provisions is prodigious; the shrill cries of those who assiduously recommend their wares, rise incessantly above the regular hubbub of the time, mixed with the still harsher screams of ballad-singers; and the frequenters of the market are seen in every quarter, hurrying to lay in materials for their Sunday dinner, and part of the supplies for the ensuing week.'

Such a vivacious scene was as familiar to Brummies of the 1920s onwards. From the old Fish Market on the corner of Bell Street, barrow boys and flower ladies stood by their hand carts and baskets, stretching down from the old Market Hall along Spiceal Street and into Jamaica Row, enticing the punters with their cries and their banter. And what names come to mind when Brummies recall the renowned traders of yesteryear – respected names like Johnnie 'The Count' Kennedy, Winnie Harte, Percy and Iris Moseley, the Ellises, the Kelly sisters and many more. On market days they were joined by country folk who came in to set up their stalls covered by tarpaulin, flogging chickens, plants and such like and spreading across from the barrow boys into the space in front of Saint Martin's. Then there were the Italian ice cream sellers, the roast chestnut and hot potato men, and the Romany wise women with their vardos – caravans – ever willing to tell your fortune.

All these were legalised traders but there were also the fly pitchers, Jack the lads who didn't have a hawker's licence and who flogged whatever they could from little suitcases – hurriedly closing them and moving on when a copper was spotted. And, of course, there were all the characters of the Bull Ring of Memory. The Andy Carrier lady, with eyes that did not see and yet with a voice recalled by generations of Brummies as she almost chirruped, 'Andy Carriers, Andy Carriers'. The escapologist who tied himself up in chains, the fire eater and sellers of patent medicines and Old Moore's Almanacks, and the strong men who flexed their muscles lifting wheels and taking blows.

A place of entertainment as much as it was of shopping, the Bull Ring also had its Speaker's Corner where orators of the stature of Percy Shurmer and Ernie McCulloch and preachers of the goodness of Holy Joe and Jimmy Jesus almost demanded that you buy a lad's gansey to help the poor and give something to Feed My Lambs. The Bull Ring of Memory. The People's Bull Ring. The pulsating heart of Brum. The Bull Ring in which the traders and the working-class shoppers mattered the most. The Bull Ring they knocked down and took from us.

Bull Street, City

Originally Bull Street was known as **Chapel Street**, after a place of worship at the Hospital of Saint Thomas The Apostle – a priory that once was recalled in the **Upper Priory** and **Lower Priory** which ran off the west and east of Old Square. Today it is brought to mind by **The Priory** close to Colmore Circus Queensway. Land for the priory was first given in 1285 by three men: the lord of the manor of Birmingham, William de Bermingham, who handed over ten acres of brushwood in Aston; Thomas of Maidenhacche, who made the same gift; and Ranulph of Rugby, who donated three acres of land in Saltley.

Over the next 25 year, a number of other local folk gave land and other sources of income to the priory. They included William of Dodeston, who allowed the priory six pence of rent in Birmingham; Nicholas in the Dale, who made over one and a half acres of land in Duddeston; Cristiana the Raggede and John of Clodeshale, each of whom handed over a cottage in Birmingham; and Roger the Moul, who gave four acres of land in Birmingham. William took his name from Duddeston; Nicholas from the dip in the land which would become Dale End; and Roger from the French word for mill which would become corrupted into Moor Street. Cristiana was one of only two women who are noted, whilst John is brought to mind today by a road in Alum Rock. (See Clodeshale Road).

The chapel of the priory, after which Chapel Street was called, was founded after grants of land and properties were made in 1351 and it became a church which was much used. However, after Henry VIII broke with the Catholic Church in the 1530s and set up the Church of England, the Hospital of Saint Thomas was dissolved along with all other priories and monasteries in the kingdom. At the same time, the chapel attached to the priory disappeared. On behalf of the king, Henry's commissioners sold the land which had belonged to these institutions. In Birmingham much of the

The junction of Bull Street and Steelhouse Lane in 1959 before these shops were demolished as part of the Inner Ring Road Scheme. Thanks to the *Birmingham Evening Mail*.

property of the Hospital of Saint Thomas was bought by the Holtes (see Holte Road). That land in the vicinity of the old priory was sold on to the Smallbrookes and then, in 1697, to John Pemberton. It was he who laid out The Square, which became the most upmarket part of Birmingham and which was to be called **Old Square**. Pemberton also cut a number of streets around The Square, one of which was called **Thomas Street** after the saint to whom the priory was dedicated. Thomas Street was swept away in the later 1800s as part of the Corporation Street Improvement Scheme.

With the disappearance of the religious order and of the chapel, the name Chapel Street dropped out of use and instead folk began to talk of Bull Street. This was because of an inn called the 'Bull' that was across the way from the old chapel and was owned by Harry Sidgwick. The inn itself was mentioned in a *Survey of the Borough and Manor or Demesne Foreign of Birmingham* which was carried out in 1553. This survey is one of the most important documents relating to the early history of Birmingham and was made following the attainder of John Dudley, Earl of Warwick and Duke of Northumberland.

Since at least 1166, the lords of the manor had been members of the de Bermingham family but the last of the line, Edward, lost his lordship to the crown in 1536. Birmingham then passed on to John Dudley, who became the country's most powerful figure during the reign of King Edward VI. After the monarch's early death, he proclaimed as queen Lady Jane Grey, the wife of his fourth son. However, Dudley was unable to stop the accession of Mary and he was executed for treason in 1553. A year later, both Lady Jane Grey and her husband were also executed. Birmingham reverted back to the crown and then was sold on to the Marrows of Berkswell. They took little interest in their manor and gradually sold off much of their land locally to people such as Bishop Sherlock, a relative of the Gooch family (see Gooch Street).

In a conjectural plan of Birmingham in 1553 that was drawn up by J. Hill, Bull Street is still shown as Chappell Street, whilst the 'Bull' inn is marked just above the Cherry Orchard which would give its name to **Cherry Street**. The importance of Bull Street as a route is shown clearly by this plan. It leads into **Sandy Lane**, later known as **Snow Hill**, and in turn this went on to become the Wolverhampton Road – today's Soho Road (see Snow Hill and Soho Road). Bull Street, then, was one of Birmingham's most important routes. It connected Digbeth with the Wolverhampton Road and so linked Brum not only with towns like Wednesbury but also with Shrewsbury and North and Mid Wales. Down this way came the Black Country coal and iron needed so much by our town's fashioners of metal and also the Welsh cattle which was so vital to feed the Brummies.

From the early 1700s, many of Birmingham's more prosperous citizens were attracted to live in the Bull Street locality. Seeking to leave the damp, crowded old town around the Bull Ring they moved up Bennetts Hill to drier and healthier spots. In particular they gathered about The Square (Old Square). This shift in population led to Bull Street becoming the main shopping centre for middle-class Brummies. Some of the Bull Street retailers achieved a high reputation. There was Benjamin Hudson, the bookseller at number 18; and next door were Thomas and William Southall the druggists, whose successors set up a factory on the Alum Rock Road. They were joined by Joseph Harris the dyer, whose firm still occupies the same address, and the Cadbury brothers. Benjamin Cadbury had a drapers at No 92; whilst in the adjoining premises, John dealt in tea before moving into the making of cocoa and chocolate. Later this shop was taken over by the Barrows, relatives of the Cadburys. They remained as provision merchants in Bull Street until the onset of supermarket shopping.

Bull Street was split into two in the early 1880s, when Corporation Street was cut as a 'Parisian style boulevard' which would reflect Birmingham's status as 'the metropolis of the Midlands'. The success of the new thoroughfare depended upon attracting important retailers, and in 1885 David Lewis opened one of his department stores on the busiest site in Corporation Street – on the corner of Bull Street. Later Grey's fancy drapers also established themselves in Bull Street, as did Rackham's. Today, Bull Street remains an important street, although the main shopping activity in Birmingham has moved to High Street and the lower ends of Bull Street, Corporation Street and New Street.

Bull Street, Harborne

In the 1850s, a builder from Coleshill called Josiah Bull York bought land in Harborne that lay off the modern High Street. Out of this estate, he cut Bull Street, **York Street** and **Josiah Street**, the name of which was changed later to **South Street**. This development was the first stage of the urbanisation of Harborne.

Burbury Street, Hockley

Little is known about the Burbury family, although in 1755 an indenture was drawn up between John Burbury and the Reverend Daniel Piercy and others regarding tenements in Cannon Street and Chapel Street.

Burlington Arcade

Formerly Burlington Passage, this name was associated with the Burlington Restaurant, which was entered down stairs and which was well-known for its Greek Cypriot staff. These provided a bridgehead for many of their felllows to immigrate to Birmingham.

C

Cadbury Road, Moseley

As with **Cadbury Drive**, Castle Vale and **Cadbury Way**, Harborne, Cadbury Road recognises the contribution made to Birmingham by the Cadburys. Hailing from the West Country, the founder of the family locally was Richard Tapper Cadbury. A Quaker, he served his apprenticeship as a draper in London and moved to Brum in 1794, setting up shop at 92 Bull Street. Successful in business, Richard played a prominent part in public life as a Street Commissioner (see Barker Street), overseer of the poor, member of the boards of various hospitals and as a promoter of the Birmingham to Derby railway line. Thirty years after he arrived in the town, his son, John, began the firm that was to make its mark upon the world when he began operating a tea shop at 93, Bull Street.

Unlike many other shopkeepers, John refused to adulterate his goods with inferior additives and soon he gained a high name. In fact his first customer was Samuel Galton of the Lunar Society and a leading citizen (see Galton Road). John was also alert to the need to show off his shop and so installed a plate glass window. This stood out from the old-fashioned green-ribbed wondows of other retailers and marked him out as progressive. The window itself was used as a display with tea chests, caddies, cone-shaped sugar loaves and Chinese vases decorated with flowers and butterflies. Inside, attention was drawn by an effigy of a Chinese man that was dressed exotically and colourfully. The tea itself was gathered in a silver scoop and weighed in brass scales suspended from the ceiling with lengthy chains.

John also sold coffee and he was attracted into the marketing of cocoa. All three products fitted in with his beliefs in non-alcoholic drinks. In 1831, John Cadbury began making his own cocoa when he rented a warehouse in Crooked Lane, which was close to the Bull Street shop. Fourteen years later his warehouse was knocked down to make way the construction of a tunnel of the Great Western Railway and he moved first to Cambridge Street and then to Bridge Street. About this time, John was joined by his brother, Benjamin, and in 1849 he passed on his shop to his nephew, Richard Cadbury Barrow. Focusing now upon the production of cocoa, the business prospered, but then entered a period of decline. In 1861, John Cadbury stepped down from the firm and it was taken on by his sons, George and Richard.

Supported strongly by their workers, the drive, determination and flair of the brothers turned things around and in 1866 they brought out a new product, Cocoa Essence. Made with no chemicals it was marketed successfully as absolutely pure. Thirteen years later, the brothers moved their factory to 'a garden' setting in Bournville. They were motivated by two things: first the need for bigger premises which allowed expansion and which had good transport links; and a desire to have their workers employed in a better environment. Here the company prospered and the Cadburys made a name not only as important businessmen but as caring employers who provided social and educational facilities for their workers. With innovative products such as Cadbury's Dairy Milk, the business continued to grow and it remains one of the most significant in Birmingham. Members of the Cadbury family have also carried on the example set by their ancestor Richard Tapper in becoming involved in public life. Today the best known member of the family is Sir Adrian, a man deeply concerned for the well being of society and a patron and supporter of numerous good causes.

California Way, California

Taking its name from the California Inn, California Way brings to the fore Isaac Flavell. He was supposed to have made something of a fortune in the California goldfields and in 1842 he bought Stonehouse Farm on the borders of Bartley Green and Harborne. With his money he is said to have built the pub. Stonehouse Farm was developed from the inter-war years. Another story goes that the area was so-named because it was as rich in clay as California was in gold and well into the twentieth century Smart's Brickworks dug out clay from the area.

California in 1949. Thanks to the *Birmingham Evening Mail*.

Camden Street, Hockley and Brookfields

In 1813, Camden Hill Villa, the home of John Pickering, was described as 'delightfully situated on Camden Hill in the neighbourhood of Lady Wood, Birmingham Heath and Soho, commanding in prospect the Dudley and Rowley Hills, Barr Beacon and an extent of rich and varied country'. By 1818 the street itself had appeared as a John Legge, builder, was mentioned as living in Camden Street. The origin of Camden Hill is not known, although a Cambden family was present in Birmingham in the eighteenth century, as indicated by a deed dated 1717 and mentioning a Henry Cambden – the man who built the mill on the Bourn Brook.

For working-class Brummies, Camden Street will always be remembered as the birthplace of Kathleen Dayus, a woman who brought to the fore the lives of her people in the back streets of Birmingham. The thirteenth child of a poor family, she grew up in a yard of back-to-backs on the edge of the Jewellery Quarter. In one of the most prosperous cities of one of the wealthiest counties in the world, the local folk had to collar and scrat for everything and anything they had.

Like Kathleen's dad, many of the chaps were out of work and were on the parish, 'but what they received was insufficient to feed us growing children, let alone our parents as well'. Friday afternoons, the hard up and unemployed would queue for cards that allowed them a bit of coal, a loaf or two, some margarine, a tin of

Camden Street, Brookfields from the corner with Ellen Street.

condensed milk, a little tea, and spoonful or so of sugar. This relief was grudging and meagre and money was never given. In their prejudice against the poor, too many of those in authority believed that poorer folk could not be trusted with cash in case they spent it on snuff, tobacco, beer or suchlike.

Poverty was a hard bed. Kathleen and her pals knew what it was to be clammed and to stand outside the factory gates begging for a piece off the workers when they knocked off. And they knew what it was like to live in tiny houses that were badly built and to have to share unsanitary dry-pan closets. As if that was not enough, Kathleen was treated harshly by her mom, a tough woman who would bounce out of the house with the old mon's flat cap pushed firmly onto her head. In later years, Kathleen came to an understanding of why her mom was that way. It was life that had squeezed the affection from her and made her forbidding.

But the life that Kathleen and her pals lived wasn't one of unremitting unhappiness. They had their laughs, they played their games, they whistled and they sang and they made the best of the bed that they lay on. Like so many Brummies who came out the back streets, Kathleen was an intelligent and persevering woman. She wanted something better out of life and through heartaches that would have broken many a person, she forged on, holding fast to a dream of a better life for her kids and a better world for her grandkids. Determined and dogged, whenever life knocked her down her pulled herself back up, dusted herself and got on with it. But Kathleen didn't just dream, she grafted to make her dream a reality. She saw her kids and grandkids – and her great grandkids – get on. But she never forgot her people. She never walked away from the working-class Brummies of the back streets and one day she set her mind to telling their tale, the tale of Her People.

In 1982 the book of that name came out. It was written with the insight and understanding of someone who belonged and who had not forgotten her roots. *Her People* was brought out by a major London publisher. It gained national attention and Kathleen went on to Terry Wogan's show. Her down-to-earth Brummie ways grabbed the audience and made them sit up and take notice. So many people wrote in to hear more of her that they had to fetch her back on. Through all the attention, Kathleen stayed the same and she wrote more books. These were also successful, but it was *Her People* that laid the ground for me and others to follow. Kathleen was the first. She was the first to recount the lives of those working-class Brummies who never had nothing from society but who gave so much. She was the pioneer and she inspired us.

I was fortunate to know Kathleen well. Fifteen years ago when I was struggling to make my way and when I had just come off the dole, she came and did a talk for me at my first teaching job. She didn't have to but she did because she wanted to help me. Kathleen was there for anyone who cared about all those Brummies whose address was back of.

Camp Hill

Old stories suggest that Prince Rupert (see Rupert Street) and his forces made their base on this hill before they attacked Birmingham in the English Civil War in 1643, hence Camp Hill recalls their camp. However, Camp Hill is really a corruption of Kempe Hill, which is mentioned in the *Archives of Rentals of King Edward's School* in 1511. **John Kempe Way** brings to mind the Kempe family, whilst nearby **Lowe Street** is named after Mr Lowe, an attorney and local landowner who lived at a house on Camp Hill called Ravenshurst, hence **Ravenshurst Street**. In 1818 he offered for sale a crop of potatoes and beans which had been grown at the top end of Bradford Street. The Lowes had a long association with the area as in 1677 a Humphrey Lowe of Coventry bequeathed Brick House Farm at Rowley Regis, let at £35 per year, to support Saint John's Chapel, Deritend. This bequest was held in trust by six inhabitants of Deritend and Bordesley. In the mid-twentieth century Camp Hill was noticeable for the Camp Hill Flyover and for a while a statue of King Kong at Camp Hill Motors. The statue is now at the market outside Edinburgh Airport.

Capern Grove, Harborne

Edward Capern, 'the poet-postman', was a post messenger in Devon and composed poems whilst trudging the lanes. In 1868 he moved to High Street, Harborne to be near his only son, and composed these lines about **Love Lane**, Edgbaston, now **Richmond Hill**: 'But no vestige of the bankside lingers now nor gate to show, The track of the old vanished lane of love's sweet long ago'.

Carey's Court

In the back-to-back court neighbourhood of working-class Brummagem, the terraces that lay off the street and were approached by an entry stood in what were called officially as courts. Most of these courts had names or numbers, but colloquially they were known as yards and many of them were given different names by their people. In Hope Street, one big yard was known as the 'Welfare Yard' because it was close to the Welfare Centre, but often the yards were known by the name of a family that had several households in it. In Our Dad's street, Studley Street, Sparkbrook, there was a 'Carey's Yard', called after a respected family headed by a wonderful old lady who was well-loved and known by all the kids of the streets as Granny Carey.

This naming tradition must have been longstanding because in one of the first directories of Birmingham in 1776, a Carey's-court is listed as coming off Moor Street. It contained one businessman, Joseph Carey a malt-mill maker. The name was abolished in 1866. The same directory also includes **Powell's-yard**, off Spicer Street (Spiceal Street), wherein was John Powell a button maker. Similarly, **Corbett's Alley** brings to mind a Robin Corbett who lived opposite High Street in the early eighteenth century. The alley ran alongside his house to a bowling green and orchard (see Cherry Street) and was later widened to become **Union Passage**.

Carless Avenue, Harborne

The Carless family was established in Harborne from at least the early sixteenth century, and in 1651 Colonel William Carless hid in Boscobel Oak with Charles II after the king's defeat at the Battle of Worcester in the Civil War. The great reformer Thomas Attwood was married to an Elizabeth Carless and later lived at The Grove in Harborne. A branch of the Carless family was well known in Birmingham from the late sixteenth century and during the Church and King Riots of 1791 (see Priestley Road) a Joseph Carless became 'a man of considerable notoriety'. A justice of the peace, he was a vehement opponent of Joseph Priestley and reformers of his ilk. With Mr Brookes (see Great Brook Street) Carless was 'responsible for the destruction of the meeting houses', and Joseph Hill and Robert K. Dent stated that it was 'owing to their action that an idle and curious crowd which gathered about the doors of the hotel on the occasion of the famous "revolution dinner" became transformed into a mob of lawless desperadoes'. Carless spent his latter days in a debtor's prison in Lichfield.

Cartland Road, Kings Heath

James Cartland was a successful Birmingham brassfounder and in 1845 he bought a house in Kings Heath called The Priory, hence **Priory Road** – which was **Station Road** until 1903. Originally it was surrounded by an estate of nine acres, but in the succeeding years this was extended to 57 acres. In 1889, Major John Howard Cartland inherited the property and improved the seventeenth-century farmhouse in which he lived and which was visited by his young relative Barbara Cartland, the novelist. Later High Sherrif of Worcestershire and regarded as the squire of Kings Heath, Cartland instructed John Bateman, an architect, to plan roads and houses on his estate. The first dwellings were erected on the corner of **Melstock Road**, although the progress of development was slow. Major Cartland's mother was Ann Howard, hence **Howard Road**, whilst **Hazelwell**, **Hazelwell Lane** and **Hazelwell Road**, Stirchley indicate the home of his brother, George, at Hazelwell Hall. The hazel well or spring, Haselwell is mentioned in the Patent Rolls in 1325.

Carrs Lane, City

According to John Alfred Langford, originally Carrs Lane was Goddes Carte Lane and was so named because it was the lane along which a cart could go to Goddes farm. By contrast Samuel Timmins believed that in the lane was kept the cart which carried the holy relics of Saint Martin's; whilst Joe McKenna states that the lane is supposed to have had the barn in which was held the mobile stage on which Medieval mystery plays were performed. McKenna adds, there is no record of such plays in Birmingham and believes that 'all we can be sure of is that Carr's Lane was once someone's cart lane'. I agree and tend to favour Langford's account, especially as in the *Letters Patent of King Edwards VI School* in 1551, Godde's Cart Lane is also given as Goode's Cart Lane.

Carver Street, Hockley

The Carvers were a prominent Birmingham family of the eighteenth and early nineteenth centuries. A Henry Carver is mentioned in a deed of 1751 and is probably the same man who was a brassfounder who owned Bromford Forge for a few years (see Bromford Lane) and was one of the first committee members of the General Hospital. The family appears to have moved into property ownership and become associated with country gentlemen. An Edward Carver was a staunch loyalist and was county steward of the Bean Club and President of the Birmingham Church and King Club. At the time of the Church and King Riots of 1791, he was one of the magistrates and gentlemen who was accused of not doing enough to stop the rioters (see also Carless Avenue, Great Brook Street and Priestley Road). Amongst the others were R. Moland, W. Digby and Robert Lawley senior and junior (see Moland Street, Digby Walk and Lawley Street). However, he was prominent in the Birmingham Volunteers and with a party of sworn constables tried to save the home of the Taylor's, of Taylor and Lloyd's Bank.

Stoddard's the famous pork butchers, on the corner of Carver Street and Icknield Street in Hockley, early 1960s.

Castle Street, City

Running parallel with Carr's Lane from High Street to Moor Street, Castle Street emerged from the coach-yard of the 'Castle' inn. It disappeared during the post-Second World War redevelopment of Birmingham, although a blocked off alley next to Littlewood's indicates where it ran. According to William Hutton, **Cannon Street** was also named after a pub and had appeared by the mid 1700s. A short and narrow

street, it was the site of the offices of the *Birmingham Evening Mail*. It still runs
between Cherry Street and New Street, parallel with Corporation Street. Similarly,
Jamaica Row (the bottom end of which once was **Balsall Street**) recalls the 'Black
Boy' and grew from that inn's coach yard. The continuation of Spiceal Street, it went
from Edgbaston Street down to Sherlock Street where it ran into Cheapside. Famed
for its barrow boys, Jamaica Row fell to the emergence of the new Bull Ring area in
the early 1960s. Lying off New Street**, Swan Passage** or Alley also took its name
from the sign of a public house. A name recorded in the sixteenth century, it was
swallowed up by Worcester Street in the 1820s.

Chad Road, Edgbaston

In Old English, ceald wella meant cold spring or stream and Chad Road is named
after the Chad Brook. At one time the junction between Francis Road and Chad Road
was known as **Good Knaves End**. One of the most famous toymakers in Britain,
Chad Valley, took its name from the locality.

Chamberlain Square, City

If Matthew Boulton bestrides the history of Birmingham in the eighteenth century,
then Joseph Chamberlain does the same in the nineteenth century. Supported actively
by a band of Liberal (later Liberal Unionist) politicians and by the majority of the
people of the city, Chamberlain's energy coursed through Brum helping to transform
it into the best-governed city in the world, as it was acclaimed by one American
journalist.

Born in 1836 in London – a connection brought to mind by his home called
Highbury in Moseley – Chamberlain was eighteen when he came to our town to keep
an eye on his father's large investment in the screw-making firm of John Nettlefold.
The Nettlefolds were close relations to the Chamberlains and young Joseph soon
took over the commercial and financial side of the business. He proved himself to be
most successful and by the 1870s, Nettlefold and Chamberlain was one of the biggest
concerns in the locality. With premises at Broad Street and Heath Street in
Smethwick it employed more than 2,500 workers.

As a Unitarian, someone who did not believe in the Trinity of God the Father,
God the Son and God the Holy Ghost, Chamberlain was motivated not only by a
desire to do well and to make money but also to work on behalf of others less
fortunate. He was profoundly affected by words of the charismatic George Dawson,
preacher at the Church of the Saviour in Edward Street, who urged better-off citizens
to enter public lfe and act for the public good. Inspired by his own beliefs and this
call to adhere to the civic gospel, Chamberlain joined others at the Unitarian Church
of the Messiah on Broad Street in teaching working men who wished to improve
their education on Sundays and weekday evenings. A passionate believer in opening
up education to everyone, in 1867, he joined George Dixon and other leading

Liberals in launching the Birmingham Educational Society. (See Dixon Road). It later merged with the National Education League and pushed for state funding for schools and a non-sectarian education.

Increasingly drawn to political action, in 1869 Chamberlain was elected to the town council. Within a short time his dynamism had gathered about him a band of sympathetic councillors and in 1873 he was elected mayor. That was no honorary title, rather it enabled Chamberlain to act decisively for the good of Birmingham. He held his office for three years and his impact was amazing. He forced through building bye-laws which effectively forbade the further building of back-to-back houses; he thrust forward sewerage and drainage schemes to make the town healthier; and he secured the passage of acts which allowed the corporation to take over the private gas and water companies, thus bringing light and fresh water to the furthest courtyard. More than this, he oversaw the bringing in of a health committee on the council to supervise and improve the public health of the town; he watched over the setting up of a municipal fire brigade; he encouraged the building of the Council House; he campaigned for the cutting of Corporation Street; and he authorised the writing of the history of the Corporation of Birmingham.

This programme of municipal socialism was led by a capitalist and entrepreneur, but Chamberlain realised that in a large urban centre, the local authority had a duty to own the utilities that were essential for the health and happiness of the citizens in general. Importantly, his municipal activity was profitable. Elected as an MP in 1876

Chamberlain Place in the 1930s. The large building at the back dominating the photo is The University of Birmingham, formerly Mason College, in Edmund Street. The old Central Library is the rounded building on the left at the top of Ratcliff Place. Thanks to Len Taylor.

for Birmingham West, Chamberlain continued to hold dear the city of his adoption and he was largely reponsible for the creation of The University of Birmingham in 1900. When he celebrated his seventieth birthday on Saturday 8 July 1906, all the factories and shops in Brum were closed and Chamberlain was acclaimed by tens of thousands of Brummies as he went on a seventeen-mile tour of the city. A few days later, he was stricken by a stroke but in the two elections of 1910 he was elected unopposed to Parliament. He died four years later in the town he loved so well. Chamberlain Square, originally Chamberlain Place, is named in honour of him. Opened in 1885, its centrepiece is the Chamberlain Memorial erected to celebrate his achievement in bringing clean water to the poor of Birmingham.

Highbury Road, Kings Heath is named after Highbury House, Chamberlain's home from 1880-1914. On the borders of Moseley and Kings Heath, the building harks back to where he came from in north London, Highbury. The house was deigned by John Henry Chamberlain, who was not a relation, and built by the Birmingham firm, John Barnsley and Sons. After Chamberlain's death in London, his son Austen gave Highbury to trustees who passed it on to the city which used it as a home for Aged Women until 1984. Today it is a magnificent conference and banqueting centre, from the balcony of which a portarit of Joseph Chamberlain seems to cast its eyes on everyone in the magnificent two-storey hall at the centre of the house. **Chamberlain Court**, off Westfield Road, is near to Highbury Park, and elsewhere in Kings Heath there is a **Chamberlain Road**.

Chapel Lane, Selly Oak

In 1829 Charles and Sarah Bridgewater came to Selly Oak for Charles to take up a job as Inspector of Tolls at the Selly Oak Locks of the Netherton and Birmingham Canal Navigation. The couple became the focus of a number who worshipped together on Sundays and started a 'Cause' by preaching services in a cottage. This cottage was the first of four adjoining the garden of the Selly Oak Cottage on the corner of Oak Tree Lane and Raddle Barn Road. It became the first chapel locally and was later knocked down to be replaced on the Bristol Road by a Wesleyan Chapel at the entrance to The Dingle and opposite Chapel Lane. **Chapel Walk**, Kings Norton is the result of the Baptist Chapel on Wharf Road. It was built in 1842 and was used by the Baptists from 1847. Because Baptists believe in a full baptism of adults, baptisms were often held in the nearby canal. In the cottage next to the chapel there lived Mrs Turner, a widow who turned the front room of her house into a sweet shop.

Chartist Road, Washwood Heath

The Great Reform Act of 1832 was a major disappointment to the working class. (See Bath Row). They had fought hard for an extension to the franchise and yet Parliament had given the vote only to middle-class men. Five years later, a number of influential men called for further political reform and put forward a six point charter: universal manhood suffrage; annual parliaments; secret ballot; abolition of property qualifications for MPs; payment of MPs; and equal electoral districts. Apart from annual parliaments, all those matters are taken for granted now but then they were regarded as radical. Thomas Attwood had led the Birmingham Political Union which had played such a vital role in the agitation for the Great Reform Act and was associated with Chartism in its early stages, presenting the movement's first petition to Parliament in 1839.

Throughout the previous year, supporters of Chartism in Birmingham had met regularly on Holloway Head and on one occasion it was estimated that 100,000 people attended. Unfortunately, there was a severe riot in July 1839. Chartists from across Britain met in Birmingham and there were great gatherings in their support. Worried, the authorities sent for police from London. The 'peelers' attacked the demonstrators and cleared the Bull Ring but then were overwhelmed in a counter attack by the Chartists. The so-called Bull Ring Riots ensued and went on for several days. This violent episode and others elsewhere cannot negate the impact of Chartism. Overall it was a peaceful movement seeking to reform and not overthrow the constitution. Chartist Road is the only road in Birmingham which brings to the fore the greatest working-class reform movement in history.

Chattaway Street, Nechells

During the late nineteenth century, one of the priests at Saint Joseph's Catholic Church, Nechells was the Reverend A.L. Chattaway. He may have given his name to this street which originally was called **Nelson Street**. However the 1873 Return of Owner's Land for Warwickshire does mention an Ann Chattaway of Aston owning 11 acres. Nechells did lie within the ancient parish of Aston, so it may be more feasible to suggest the naming of Chattaway Street after this woman and her family – to whom the priest may or may not have been related. The street was cut out in 1884.

Cheapside, Deritend

Hutton states that Cheapside recalls its counterpart in London, but the location of the street suggests that those who named it were doing so because of Birmingham connotations. The Old English word ceping or cieping meant a market and in Birmingham it was used in **Corn Cheaping** to indicate where the sellers of corn gathered close to Saint Martin's in the Bull Ring. Corn Cheaping was of great age, and is noted in a deed from 1685. It disappeared in 1806 when the Bull Ring was opened up by the Street Commissioners. The schedule for the work to widen the market place mentions clearing four messuages or tenements adjoining and fronting to the Corn Market. (See Bull Ring). Cheapside was a continuation of Jamaica Row which ran into Spiceal Street and the heart of the markets or ceping. It is mentioned first in 1781, when an early building society published plans for its extending its length along with those of Birchall Street, Bradford Street, Lombard Street and Moseley Street.

The corner of Cheapside and Alcester Street in the late 1940s. The shop on the corner is that of Florence May Hales. It is followed by a Wimbush bread shop, the greengrocery of Frank Allcot, the newsagent's of Mrs Edith Bishop and the 'Rose and Crown'. Saint Anne's Roman Catholic Church is in the background.

Cherry Street, City

Cherry Street was apparent by Bradford's map of 1750 and took its name from Walker's Cherry Orchard whiich lay between Temple Row, Bull Street, High Street, New Street and Needless Alley. According to *Showell's Dictionary*, at the end of the eighteenth century it was still a 'large and fruitful orchard' which was a favourite spot. **Cherrywood Road**, Bordesley Green once was **Wood Lane** and although it was un-named, was apparent on *Tomlinson's Survey* of Bordesley in 1760. The bend in the modern road was the exact spot that was the boundary between the manors of Saltley and Bordesley.

Chester Road, various

This was the main road from London to the north west and in 1745 along it passed the army of the Duke of Cumberland on its way to engage Bonnie Prince Charlie. The historian of Erdington, William Fowler, remembered that in his youth in the mid-1800s, it was common to see to see droves of cattle numbering hundreds going along the Chester Road.

Cheston Road, Nechells

The 1873 Return of Owner's Land for Warwickshire notes that the executors of Charles Cheston of Aston owned 23 acres of land worth £185. Given that Nechells was in the parish of Aston and that the district of Aston was just across the canal from Cheston Road, it is likely that the road is named after this man.

Chinnbrook Road, Billesley

The story in my family is that the Chinn Brook was named after one of my ancestors who worked on the Cartland Estate in the Kings Heath area and who lived by this stream. Well, my grandad's grandfather did work on the land in that locality in the mid-nineteenth century, as had done his father, but the name Chinn Brook predates the presence of my family by hundreds of years. A grant of land by King Offa to Worcester Cathedral mentions property in Kings Norton, to which Kings Heath belonged, and the ciondan and ceondan. The same names occur in a document from 972 which refers to Yardley, through the easternmost edge of which the Chinn Brook flows. In the *Place Names of Worcestershire* it is stated that 'from the bounds from which the first forms come it may be inferred that ciondan is a stream name'. If this is the case, ciondan was the Chinn Brook. In the succeeding centuries, the name was given as Chende (1255), Chwyndes (1425) and Chyndehouse (1642). The modern Chinnbrook Road emerged in the 1920s with the development of the Yardley Wood and Billesley municipal estates.

Christchurch Passage, City

Sited on an angle between Colmore Row and New Street, Christchurch was built in 1805. It was paid for by public subscription on land given by W. P. Inge (see Inge Street). The church and its site were sold in 1895, the proceeds from which helped found Saint Agatha's, Sparkbrook. Demolished in 1899, the church was recalled by Christchurch Passage that ran down from Waterloo Street into New Street. The name went with the redesign of Victoria Square in the late twentieth century.

Church Avenue, Moseley

Church Avenue, Moseley is across the road from Saint Mary's, Moseley; whilst **Church Road**, Moseley was part of Ladypool Lane until 1855. For centuries Moseley was in the parish of Kings Norton, but distant as it was from the church of Saint Nicolas its people sent a petition to Pope Innocent VII saying that for old men, pregnant women and other weak persons access to Kings Norton was impossible, especially during floods. In 1405 the Pope mandated the Bishop of Worcester to licence a chapel at ease in Moseley. Then in 1494-5, Elizabeth of York, the lord of the manor of Kings Norton and wife of Henry VII, made a grant of waste lands as a site for a chapel. Little is known of any building until 1513 when mention is made of the construction of a steeple at Moseley dedicated to Our Lady, Saint Mary. The rest of the modern church dates from alterations and extensions in the nineteenth and twentieth centuries. Joseph Lucas is buried in the churchyard.

Church Lane, **Church Hill Road**, **Church Avenue** and **Church Vale** Handsworth are named after Saint Mary's Church on the Hamstead Road. It has roots as far back as 1200 when a priest was mentioned as serving there. Indeed, the lower part of the south tower dates to the late twelfth or early thirteenth centuries, and the upper part to the fifteenth century. The church was extended by 1821 and in 1876-80 the fourteenth-century south aisle was rebuilt. By this time, the growth of Handsworth, meant that various new parishes had been created out of that of Saint Mary. The three great industrialists, Matthew Boulton, James Watt and William Murdock are buried at Saint Mary's.

Church Road and **Church Hill**, Northfield connect with Saint Laurence, the parish church of Northfield. It is another notable place of worship which is long established. The Domesday Book entry for Northfoeld 1086 notes a priest, and it is believed that the stone for the church built in the mid-1100s was taken from a quarry which is recalled in **Quarry Lane**. The chancel was added between 1200 and 1214 and the south aisle in the fourteenth century. Enlarged with a north aisle at the end of the nineteenth century and graced by a peel of eight bells since 1927, the church has a Norman doorway, a hidden staircase and the 'leper's squint'. This is a small opening, now filled in, and was thought to have allowed lepers to look in the church.

Church Road, Yardley and its continuation **Church Lane**, Kitts Green are bonded with Saint Edburgha, Yardley. Dedicated to the grand-daughter of King Alfred the Great, folklore has it that some of her relics are in the church. There is

Church Hill, Northfield, with the church of Saint Laurence on the right, about 1920s.

documentary evidence of a chapel from the later twelfth century, but the earliest part of the church is from the thirteenth century. Much of the exterior remains as it would have been when the church was rebuilt in the fourteenth and fifteenth centuries. Saint Edburga's was the burial place of the Hay family, brought to mind in Hay Mills, and the Este family (see Este Road). In the adjoining district is **Church Road**, Sheldon, telling of Saint Giles's, the parish church. Its nave goes back to about 1330 and much of the rest of the church is from the later Middle Ages. Like the other Medieval churches of Birmingham, it is in a rural setting amidst urban development.

In Edgbaston, **Church Road** indicates the district's parish church of Saint Bartholomew. Originally a chapel of Harborne it is mentioned first in 1279, and as a parish church in 1658. By this date it had been damaged badly in the English Civil War and after a large-scale fundraising exercise it was rebuilt. Enlarged in the nineteenth century, it includes various monuments to the Gough family and Dr William Withering, the man who discivered digitalis and a key figure in the beginnings of the Birmingham General Hospital.

Erdington also has a **Church Road**, leading to Saint Barnabas on the High Street and consecrated in 1824 and hence also **Barnabas Road**; as does Perry Barr, where the **Church Road** heads to Saint John of the Evangelist, opened for worship in 1833. Elsewhere there is a **Church Street** in Lozells, (see Saint Silas Square); a **Church Walk** in Ward End (see Saint Margaret's Road); and an **Old Church Road** and an **Old Church Avenue**, Harborne (see Saint Peter's Road). **Church Street** in the city is named after Saint Philip's Church and connects Great Charles Street and Colmore Row. It was apparent by Bradford's Map of 1750 (see Inge Street).

Churchill Road, Bordesley Green

In 1899, the United Kingdom went to war with the Boer Republics of the Transvaal and the Orange Free State in what is now South Africa. The Boers were descendants of Dutch and Huguenot (French Protestant) settlers and put up a fierce resistance to the British forces. Many people saw the British action as wrong and it caused great controversy at the time. It was a long and bloody conflict and the Boers had a number of successes which shocked the British, especially in the first year. The then Winston Churchill reported on the war but was captured by the enemy. Daringly he escaped and his exploits on his way to freedom enthralled people at home. In Birmingham, Churchill Road was named in his honour as it was cut out soon after the Boer War which ended in 1901.

Other roads locally also recall the Boer War: **Colonial Road** and **Imperial Road** emphasise that the Boer republics became colonies of the British Empire; **Pretoria Road** is named after the capital of the Transvaal, which became the administrative capital of South Africa; and **Botha Road** stresses the South African statesman and soldier Louis Botha. He was Commander in Chief of the Boer forces from 1900, but after the defeat of his people he worked strenuously for reconciliation. In 1907 he

Looking down Churchill Road, Bordesley Green in the early 1900s.

became Prime Minister of the Transvaal and three years later was elected premier of the new Union of South Africa. During the First World War Botha led the conquest of German South West Africa. He was much admired in Britain.

Across the city in Rotton Park, just off Shenstone Road, is **Colenso Road**. This commemorates the Battle of Colenso in the Boer War in December 1899 and at which a British force intent upon relieving the siege of Ladysmith was beaten. At this battle a Birmingham man called George Ravenhill won the Victoria Cross, the United Kingdom's highest award for valour. Born in Nechells in 1872, he joined the Royal Scots Fusiliers aged seventeen and served for six years. George then re-enlisted in 1899. The citation for his VC reads:

> Private Ravenhill left his sheltered position several times during the 15th December 1899 at Colenso, under extremely heavy fire, to assist the officers and drivers trying to withdraw several guns of the Royal Field Artillery, when the personnel serving them had been killed, wounded or driven back by infantry fire from point-blank range. He helped limber up one of the guns that were saved.

Later a prisoner of war of the Boers, George was not well treated after he returned to civilian life. He did not receive his £50 per year war pension and from 1902 until 1908 was given only £20. That year he was stripped of his medal for stealing a few shillings worth of scrap iron. He was the last man to have this done to him. As his great grandson Matthew Ravenhill stresses, his descendants 'still feel deeply uspet that he is portrayed as a "Rogue" over 100 years later'. He acknowledges that George was no angel but believes passionately that his relative's name should be cleared.

My family and I know the truth. He was a family man who served his Country and Birmingham with undescribeable valour and was forced to petty crime and forfeiting his VC in order to provide for his family, which to this day was equally as courageous as his act performed at the Battle of Colenso.

George's hardships are made plain by the fact that his son, Alfred, was born in Erdington Workhouse and it is apparent that his difficult circumstances were realised by his fellow Brummies. When he died in 1921, a large crowd lined the streets of Nechells to pay their respects to him. He should be better honoured today for his sake and that of his family.

Running from Colenso Road is **Majuba Road**, recalling the first Boer War of 1880-1. In 1877, the British had annexed the bankrupt Boer Republic of the Transvaal, but in December 1880 the Boers rose up in revolt. On 27 February 1881 a small British force was defeated at Majuba Hill, after which the government of Gladstone decided to withdraw from the Transvaal, the independence of which was recogised a year later.

Clapgate Lane, Bartley Green and Woodgate Valley

Donald Wright believes that this is surely from a clapper-gate, one side of which collapses as it is pressed upon – thus allowing a person to step over it. Once this was done the gate returns to its original position.

Clay Lane, South Yardley

Vivian Vird felt that this road is named after Henry Clay, acclaimed by Robert K. Dent as a 'hero of the workshop'. A former apprentice to Baskerville, Clay patented the making of papier maché in 1772. The product was made by pasting several layers of paper upon the sides of boards of a regular thickness. These were then moulded, dried on a hot stove and rubbed or dipped in oil and varnish. Once finished the papier maché could be sawn, planed or turned like wood and be japanned. It was used for making tables, snuff boxes, tea trays and panels for doors, coaches and sedans. The trade became a major one in Birmingham until fashion changes led to its end. Clay himself became a wealthy man and gained the status of High Sheriff of Warwickshire. Vivian Bird mentions that some of Clay's wares were on show in Blakesley Hall, Yardley but I find the connection with Henry Clay too tenuous and would suggest that the road was once close to clay pits.

Claybrook Street, City

Now just a cut through between Hurst Street and Bromsgrove Street, this was formerly the **Pudding Brook** mentioned in the song 'I Can't Find Brummagem'. Hutton described the strange nature of the brook:

Near the place where this small rivulet discharges itself into the moat (see Moat Lane) another of the same size is carried over it, called Pudding Brook, and proceeds from the town as this advances towards it, producing a curiosity seldom met with. One river runneth south, and another north, for half a mile, yet only a path of three feet asunder, which surprised Brindley, the famous engineer.

Going across Bradford Street, Pudding Brook was overwhelmed by the growth of Birmingham and was last mentioned in an advertisement in 1815. Its name related to the nature of the ground near it, also reflected in the calling of Claybrook Street.

Clayton Road, Saltley

One of the most famous canal carriers of all was the firm of Fellows, Morton and Clayton. Their name can be seen still emblazoned on the outside of their premises in Fazeley Street. The company also had docks at Saltley where narrow boats were made and repaired and which were close to Clayton Road. Thomas Clayton, third son of William Clayton of Saltley, lived at the Cedars, Castle Bromwich, hence **Clayton Drive** and **Cedar Avenue**, where he was active in the local community.

Clissold Close, Balsall Heath

The late grandmother of Denise Meredith used to talk about her sister, Rose Clissold, who was brought up in Balsall Heath and who had a feisty past. She had been blacked by a lot of firms because she tried to unionise the workforce wherever she was employed. Rose also worked a lot for the late Dennis Howell MP. The family believes that Clissold Street is called after Rose.

Clodeshall Road, Alum Rock

Located in the old manor of Saltley, Clodeshall Road commemorates the de Clodeshale family of the Middle Ages. A Walter de Clodeshale was a wealthy citizen locally and in 1331 he endowed Clodeshale's Chantry in Saint Martin's Church. The next year he bought the manor of Saltley. His son, Richard, added to the endowment so as to support a second priest to pray for him and his wife. The last male member of the family married a daughter of the Middlemores of Edgbaston (see Middlemore Road) and after his death Saltley Manor passed to his daughter, Elizabeth Clodeshale who was married to Robert Arden (see Arden Road).

Cockshut Hill, Yardley

Noted as Cokeshotefeld in 1457, this was the place (shut) where woodcocks (cock) or pigeons were trapped. It is best known today for its secondary school.

Cofton Road, Longbridge

First mentioned as Coftune in the eighth century, Cofton means a farmstead with a hut or shelter. In 930 the area was given by King Athelstan to Saint Mary's Church,

Worcester and in the Domesday Book of 1086 it was recorded as Costune, a berwick of Alvechurch Manor. It remains outside Birmingham. From the twelfth century, the estate was held by the Haket family. By 1437 the locality was known as Corfton Hakett and it kept this name although later it was owned by the Joliffes. Charles I is supposed to have stopped at Cofton Hacket Hall after Hawkesley Hall was taken by the Parliamentarians in 1645. So loyal to the king was the Joliffe of that time, that it is told that he was given a key to visit Charles when he was imprisoned. Faithful to the last, Joliffe attended the execution of his monarch.

Colebrook Road, Greet

The River Cole is brought to mind by a number of roads: **Colebourne Road** and **Cole Meadow Road**, Billesley; **Cole Bank Road** and **Cole Valley Road**, Hall Green; and **Cole Hall Lane**, Shard End (recalling Cole Hall Farm). The place name expert, E. Ekwall, feels that Cole might come from coll, a Celtic word meaning hazel. Another authority, Kenneth Cameron, agrees that it might mean a river abounding in hazels. However, in his important work on place names A. D. Mills believes that the origin is uncertain even though Cole would seem to be a pre-English word. Whatever the case, the name is indicated as early as 799 when mention is made of Colleshyl, Coleshill, the hill above the Cole.

Coleridge Passage, City

A short passage between Steelhouse Lane and Corporation Street and by the Law Courts, this brings to the fore Judge David Coleridge. It was made in 1891.

Coleshill Street, Gosta Green

There is evidence of a road to Coleshill from the mid 1400s and in the first plan of Birmingham surveyed by Westley in 1731, Coleshill Street is shown on the north-eastern edge of the town and leading to fields.

College Road, various

During his time as pastor at the Ebenezer Chapel in Steelhouse, the Reverend Timothy East (see Alfred Street, Sparkbrook) suggested to George Storer Mansfield that there was a need for the building of a college in which men could be trained for the ministry as Congregationalists. For this purpose, Mansfield gave properties to the Spring Hill Charity and in 1838 his sisters handed over their house in Spring Hill to be a college. Nineteen years later, Spring Hill College was moved to a superb building in Wake Green, Moseley. At the end of the nineteenth century the institution was relocated to Mansfield College, Oxford. Spring Hill College, however, is remembered by a **College Road**, Brookfields and **College Road**, Moseley.

    College Road, Quinton recalls Bourne College, a private school for sons of gentlemen and in 1968 in the *Birmingham Post*, Beryl Cutler recollected that at the

The junction of College Road, Moseley and the Stratford Road with Tenby Road on the right, 1938. Thanks to the *Birmingham Evening Mail*.

start of the twentieth century there were many black students – 'an unusual sight to us in Quinton in those days'. **College Road**, Handsworth Wood leads to the Wesleyan Theological College, now part of City College, the coat of arms of which included the cassowary. This was an ostrich-like bird and gave rise to **Cassowary Road**. **College Road**, Alum Rock brings to mind the Church of England run Saltley College for the Training of Teachers – later Saltley College. Finally, **College Road**, Kingstanding leads to the Roman Catholic Oscott College. It moved here from Old Oscott in 1838.

Colmore Row and Colmore Circus, City

The Colmore family owned wide lands in Birmingham and are recalled in a number of roads. There is a tradition that originally they were Huguenots, Protestants who fled religious persecution in France in the seventeenth century. This is incorrect as the family was present locally before the Reformation. In his book on Birmingham, Vivian Bird mentions that the Colmores originated from Tournai in France – but I have been unable to corroborate this suggestion. Whatever the origins of the family, it appears that the Colmores emerged in Birmingham in the early sixteenth century, as none of them are mentioned in deeds before that time. In 1525, a deed of release was drawn up from Henry Colmer to William Colmer, both of Birmingham, in respect of tenements in Dale End and it would seem that from an early date the Colmores bought lands with their profits from trading.

A magnificent photo by Mike Cann of Colmore Row in June 1953 at the time of the Coronation Parade. Thanks to the family of Mike Cann.

In 1584, another document named a William Colmore as a mercer – someone who dealt in fabrics, especially silk and other costly materials. Four years later he was one of only three men in Birmingham to pay £25 as a loan to Queen Elizabeth when a Spanish Invasion was feared at the time of the Spanish Armada. The importance of the family is indicated elsewhere. In 1551, King Edward VI endowed a Free Grammar School in Birmingham. He did this with part of the property which had belonged to the Guild of the Holy Cross, a religious insitution which had been put down when Henry VIII dissolved the monasteries in 1536. Based in New Street for hundreds of years, the school is now in Edgbaston, across the way from The University of Birmingham. (See also King Edward's Place). When Edward VI established the school he named a number of significant local men as 'Gouvernors of the possessions Revenewes and goodes of the seyd free grammer Schoole'. Amongst these notables were both William Colmore the elder and William Colmore the younger.

The older William Colmore died in 1566 and was remembered by a slab in Saint Martin's Church and upon which he was shown in a long civilian's gown, with hanging sleeves – each of which had slits at the upper part and through which the arms passed. That slab disappeared and today one of the oldest memorials in our parish church is one that is of dark wood and is high on the south transept wall. It was erected in 1612 by William Colmore in memory of his parents and shows the 'Grim Reaper' – a seated skeleton holding a scythe.

By the seventeenth century, it is likely that the Colmores had ceased to be merchants and now were living off their properties. Probably in the reign of James I, the Colmores erected their residence at New Hall, hence **Newhall Hill**, Hockley and **Newhall Street**, Hockley. For a time in the 1700s the bottom end of Newhall Street was known as **Mount Street** and the top end as **Newport Street**. It is likely that the hall itself was approached from gates which stood at what is today the junction of Newhall Street and Great Charles Street. In 1754 an advertisement stated that New Hall was 'near Birmingham', but as Francis White put it expressively in 1850, Birmingham was a speedy traveller and 'marched over the premises, and covered them with twelve hundred houses, on building leases'.

The development of the New Hall estate was presaged in 1746 when an act of Parliament empowered Ann, widow of Charles Colmore, to make building leases. She gave her name to **Ann Street**, formerly **Mount Pleasant**. This was a high point on the ridge above Birmingham and gave lovely views. It went in front of what became the Council House and in 1881 it was swallowed up by **Colmore Row**. This name had emerged two years before when the building of a grand Council House led to the replacement of **Monmouth Street**. Itself named only in 1850, Monmouth Street ran from Bull Street to Newhall Street. Previously this stretch of Colmore Row had also been called **Bull Lane** and before that **Newhall Lane**.

Six years after the act of 1746, Ann Colmore was leasing land in **Edmund Street**, called after her younger brother-in-law and known until 1778 as **Harlow Street**. By Hanson's Map of 1778, **Charles Street** and **Great Charles Street** were also obvious – named after Ann's husband and one of her sons – as was **Lionel Street**. This referred to one of Ann's grandchildren, as did **Mary Ann Street** and **Caroline Street**. By 1787, her son, Charles Colmore, was leasing land in Saint Paul's Square and it was he who had given the ground for the church. As Hawkes Smith pointed out in 1825, 'such donations, though beneficial, are not quite disinterested; for the erection of a Chapel or a Church, produces an immediate crop of houses around it, and the land, from paying an agricultural rent, is soon many times doubled in value, by being let by the yard, and paying a building rent'. Another name associated with the Colmores is **Eden Place**. Going alongside the Council House between Colmore Row and Edmund Street, it recalls Dr Thomas Eden who married into the Colmores. For many years, Eden Place was associated with a blind painter who plied his trade at the Colmore Row end.

The development of the New Hall Estate was crucial in the urbanisation of Birmingham. It was a large plot of land upon which were built good quality houses for the affluent middle class. In the the early to mid-1800s, these better-off folk were mostly pulled away to the emerging fashionable suburb of Edgbaston and their former homes were subdivided into premises for people involved in the jewellery trade – whilst, the large gardens were built over with 'shopping' (workshops) and back-to-back houses. From the later 1700s, streets were also cut through another of the estates owned by the Colmores – that land which lay north of Tower Street in Hockley (see Farm Street).

Charles Colmore died in 1794 and his estate passed to his only surviving son, Lionel, who died in 1807 without any heirs. The Colmore properties were inherited by his sister, Caroline. According to the will of Charles, if his heirs died without issue then his lands would go to his 'dear friend', Francis, Lord Hertford of Ragley Hall in Alcester – or to that man's son, Lord Yarmouth, and in 1829, the Colmore Estate was divided between Caroline and the grandson of Lord Hertford. Eight years later, Caroline died in Cheltenham and her share of the property was willed to her friend Frind Cregoe – so long as he took the name of Colmore.

The Cregoes were Cornish, hence **Cornwall Street** which until 1898 was **Bread Street**. During the mid 1800s, the Cregoes allowed development on their Bell Barn Estate, thus **Bellbarn Road**, where **Cregoe Street** and **Great Colmore Street** remember them. In 1857, Frind's son, Colmore Frind Cregoe-Colmore, sold the site of the Council House to the Corporation for £33,000. The family also leased for 999 years the site of the Council House extension and gave the land for the School of Art in Margaret Street. Colmore' son was William Barwick Cregoe-Colmore, hence **Barwick Street**, whilst **Margaret Street** is called after his sister. The male line of the Cregoe-Colmores died out with William in 1918 and to pay the death duties, tenants were allowed to buy much of the property on both the Bell Barn and Oozells estates (see also Oozells Street). Today, the remainder of the Colmore estate belongs to descendants of William's three sisters. They live in various parts of the world.

Colmore Crescent, Moseley brings to mind Canon Colmore, a relation of the Colmores and vicar of Saint Mary's Church, Moseley between 1876-1907. As Moseley's population expanded he wanted to see a new church for the Wake Green area and achieved his aim with the consecration of Saint Agnes Church in 1884. It was named after his wife and was sited in **Colmore Crescent**, known as **Saint Agnes Crescent** until 1907 when it was renamed in honour of the Canon.

Colonnade Passage, City
Named after the Colonnade Hotel, which later became the Chamber of Commerce, Colonnade Passge went between the hotel and the Theatre Royal at the top end of New Street and into Stephenson Street. It was demolished in 1961.

Conybere Street, Highgate
Meaning the rabbits (coney) in the barley (bere), Conybere Street is just one of scores of Brummagem street names which remind us of the countryside. It runs west and

Colonnade Passage in 1961. Thanks to the *Birmingham Evening Mail*.

downhill from the high ground of the Moseley Road to Gooch Street in the valley of the River Rea. For centuries the land hereabouts was part of the hamlet of Deritend, belonging to the manor of Bordesley in the parish of Aston. In 1730 it was bought by Dr Thomas Sherlock, Bishop of Bangor and later of London, who owned substantial property nearby and who passed it on to the Gooch family (see Gooch Street). Squashed between Darwin Street, Belgrave Road, the River Rea and the Moseley

Road, the Conybere Street area was still mostly agricultural in 1838 when it was swallowed up by a land-hungry Brum. From 1881 the district has been dominated by the superb church of Saint Alban the Martyr, designed by J. L. Pearson, and a leading centre of High Church of England worship. Latterly the area's skyline has also been graced by the nearby Central Mosque in Belgrave Road, sited on the former Dare's Brewery.

Similarly, **Congreve Street** recalls the rabbit warren belonging to the priory of the Hospital of Saint Thomas (see Bull Street). This was recorded in a document from 1532 as the Conyngre and it covered 160 acres on the western side of the lands of the Priory. The street was called **Friday Street** until 1779, supposedly because it was here on Fridays that masters paid their workmen. Today Congreve Street has shrunk to **Congreve Passage** alongside the Central Library.

Congreve Street in 1936, showing old buildings soon to be demolished. Thanks to the *Birmingham Evening Mail*.

Cook Street, Nechells

Formerly **Trafalgar Road**, as on *Pigott Smith's Map* of 1855, this street became Cook Street in 1880, perhaps recalling William Cook who was a prominent Birmingham politician. Born in Stroud, Gloucestershire, he was eight when he came to Birmingham with his parents. A skilled worker, when he was twenty he joined the

Amalgamated Society of Engineers, becoming a union official and then a councillor in 1873. The following year he was chosen as chairman of the Health Committee and was re-elected as such for many years. Under his chairmanship, the borough hospital was erected and a disinfecting station was started. Cook became mayor in 1883 and was a member of Parliament for Birmingham for one year following his election in 1885. After Joseph Chamberlain split with the William Gladstone and the Liberals in 1886, Cook remained a strong Gladstonian.

William Cook Road, Ward End is certainly named after this man and the developer of this area must have had strong Liberal sympathies, for it also boasts an **Asquith Road** and a **Morley Road**. Herbert Henry Asquith, the 1st Earl of Oxford, hence **Oxford Close**, was born in Morley, West Yorkshire. A lawyer, he entered Parliament for East Fife in 1886 as a Liberal, becoming Chancellor of the Exchequer in 1905 and prime minister three years later. Asquith headed a reforming government that limited the power of the House of Lords and brought in the National Insurance Act. He was faced with several crises, with regards to the suffragette movement, Home Rule for Ireland and the First World War. In 1915, Asquith formed a colaition government but was ousted a year later in favour of Lloyd George. He was defeated in the election of 1918, returning two years later. His disputes with Lloyd George and changing socio-economic conditions led to the decline of the Liberal Party.

Cope Street, Spring Hill

A John Cope was one of the first Street Commissioners in 1769, whilst in 1813, Charles and John Cope were elected governors of King Edward's School. *Wrightson's Directory* of 1818 gives Charles as a brass founder and caster in general in John Street, and John and Charles as military cabinet and coach brass founders in Fleet Street. John had houses on Hagley Row (now Road) and Summer Hill Terrace, close to Spring Hill and this fact accounts for the nearby Cope Street, which emerged in 1882.

Coralie Street, Brookfields

Margaret Read, nee Morris, tells me that Coralie Street and the nearby Rosalie Street were believed to have been named after two of the daughters of the builder of the area. They were pronounced as Co-ra-lea and Rose-a-lea, with the accent on the 'e' in 'lea'. Margaret wonders how two pretty names became so mispronounced.

Corn Exchange, City

Located off High Street, this passage led to the Corn Exchange that was opened in 1847 and which replaced the corn market that had been held in and about the Bull Ring for centuries. The passage was demolished in the 1930s.

Coronation Road, Bournbrook and Washwood Heath

Called **Selly Park Station Road** until 1902, Coronation Road, Bournbrook and its counterpart in Washwood Heath celebrated the coronation of King Edward VII, who succeeded Queen Victoria in 1901.

Corporation Street, City

As mayor, Joseph Chamberlain had a vision of making Birmingham a pre-eminent city state (see Chamberlain Square). As part of that vision he wanted to clear some of the worst slums in the town and cut 'a Parisian-style boulevard which would reflect Birmingham's status as 'the metropolis of the Midlands'. To further his idea, he succeeded in obtaining government permission for an Improvement Scheme. This was to run uphill from New Street to Aston Street and was to be named after the Corporation itself. Demolitions began in August 1879 in New Street, opposite Stephenson Place, but work was not completed until the turn of the twentieth century. The scheme did rid the city of much unfit property, but it attracted criticism because it failed to address the needs of the poor whose homes were lost.

Looking up Corporation Street in the 1950s, with Lewis's up on the left and the Central Methodist Hall in the background. This is another smashing photo by Mike Cann, courtesy of his family.

A major new shopping thoroughfare was created which also boasted leading stores such as Lewis's and impressive public buildings like the Victoria Law Courts. But new housing was not provided until 1890 and 1891 – and that was both too little for the numbers who had been moved out and too expensive for them. Amongst the streets cleared for Corporation Street were **Thomas Street**, **John Street**, **Lichfield Street** and **Stafford Street**. From the mid-1800s, large numbers of Irish folk from Roscommon and Mayo had settled here. As with improvement schemes elsewhere in the country, the development of a middle-class shopping thoroughfare was paid for by the destruction of poorer working-class neighbourhoods.

Cotteridge Road, Cotteridge
The first indication of Cotteridge is given in 1317 when the Patent Rolls mention a Hugh de Cotteruge who is likely to have taken his name from the area in which he lived. Cotteridge belonged to Kings Norton and it is probable that it means Cotta's Ridge, and indeed there is a clear ridge running up from Breedon Hill. Other less likely explanations suggest that Cotteridge may have been where cottars lived – farm labourers who had a cottage; or else that it is derived from the village of Cotteridge elsewhere in Worcestershire. Cotteridge Road takes its name from the district.

Cotton Lane, Moseley
In 1766, a builder and timber merchant called George Cotton bought the lease of some land in Moseley. His family was noticeable in the district well into the nineteenth century.

Court Road, Sparkhill
Known as **Little Showell Green Lane** until 1899, Court Road, Sparkhill brings to mind the Police Court that was held at the back of Sparkhill Police Station. **Court Road**, Balsall Heath refers to the Police Court at Edward Road Police Station.

Court Oak Road, Harborne,
This recalls a wood in Harborne that was destroyed in the mid-1800s.

Coventry Road, various
Mentioned in a document from 1346 as the road 'from Burmyngeham to Coventre', the Coventry Road probably was in use from at least the 1200s. It was turnpiked between 1745 and 1851when Birmingham took over its maintenance.

Cowper Street, Summer Lane
William Cowper or Cooper was associated with the Aston Furnace which stood at the corner of Porchester Street and Furnace Lane and which was noted first in 1615. This was not a mill rather it was a place where the water from Hockley Brook was

used to work the furnace. Later used by the Jennens family in connection with Bromford Forge (see Jennens Row and Bromford Lane), the building was used until 1865 and gave its name to the strangely-shaped and narrow **Furnace Lane** which survived into the twentieth century and which ran from half way up Porchester Street to Gower Street, Lozells. Cowper Street was just down Summer Lane from Porchester Street and was called **Phillip Street** until 1881.

Cox Street West, Balsall Heath

Both Cox Street West and **Upper Cox Street** lay in the Longmoors, hence **Longmoor Street**. This was the estate in the valley of the Rea which was liable to flooding and which was mentioned in 1608. It was owned by Dr John Cox, chaplain of Deritend, and was sold off for building in 1869. The Cox family played an important role locally. Dr Edward Townsend Cox, a noted surgeon, was influential in the move to build Saint Paul's Church on the Moseley Road; whilst his son, William Sands Cox, left many charitable legacies. These included £3,000 to help build and endow Saint Thomas in the Moors Church in Balsall Heath and £12,000 to erect and endow three dispensaries in Aston, Hockley and Sherbourne Road, Balsall Heath. Sands Cox was a noted doctor and was crucial in setting up the Birmingham Royal School of Medicine and Surgery in 1828. This became Queen's College in 1843 and as such it was a forerunner of The University of Birmingham.

Cranemoor Street, Nechells

According to *John Tomlinson's Map* of Saltley in 1760, Crane Moor was in Saltley, above the River Rea and just below Washwood Heath. This location is confirmed by a map of 1899 which indicates that **Arley Road**, Saltley was **Cranemoor Lane** – although officially the name had been changed two years previously. Across the Rea from this spot was cut Cranemoor Street, Nechells.

The Crescent

In 1778, a Charles Norton decided to develop a crescent of high quality houses at the back of Broad Street. A lack of investment meant that this ambitious plan for The Crescent led to the building of only twelve houses, the last of which were knocked down in the 1960s when The Crescent and Crescent Wharf disappeared. The street is remembered in the name of the 'Crescent Theatre' in Sheepcote Street. Originally part of The Crescent, **Cambridge Street** emerged in the 1790s and by the turn of the nineteenth century it had gained its own name.

Crockets Road, Handsworth

In researching his family history, Jack Crockett found that his Crockett ancestors were benefactors to the local community. A Thomas Crockett was the keeper of the 'New Inn' on the Holyhead Road in the later 1700s. His son, John, followed his father as a publican, became an overseer of the poor and gave land for a chapel of ease, thus leading to **Chapel Street**. This became the church of Saint James. In Frederick Hackwood's history of Handsworth (1908), John Crockett was praised as a gentlemanly host of the old school who conducted his public house more like a private house.

Croft Road, Yardley
Originally this was **Moses Lane**.

Crooked Lane, City
By 1750, this had emerged out of the **Lamb Yard** beside Lamb House on the corner of High Street and Bull Street. An alleyway running from the top of Martineau Street to the bottom of that same street, it was crooked and was used as a short cut into Union Passage and cut through to New Street. It disappeared in the redevelopments of the early 1960s to make way for the an island. The last folk to live in the Lamb House were the Suffields. They ran a hosiery and lace business and were the maternal grandparents of the author and scholar of Anglo-Saxon, J.R.R. Tolkien (see Sarehole Road). The first editions of the *Evening Mail* (then called the *Birmingham Daily Mail*) were published at 4, Crooked Lane on 7 September 1870.

Crooked Lane in 1959. Thanks to the *Birmingham Evening Mail*.

Cross Street, Gosta Green

Leading off Coleshill Street, Cross Street went over Tanter Street and ran parallel with Stafford Street. According to *Westley's Map* of 1731, Stafford Street was known also as **The Butts** and on Joseph Hill's Conjectural Plan of Birmingham in 1553, the land hereabouts was marked as Colmore's Tanter Fields or Tanter Buttes The Butts was a place on the edge of a settlement where men practiced their archery, when it was compulsory to do so in the Middle Ages, by shooting at butts. Just over what became Aston Street lay the Cross Fields. By Bradford's Map of 1750, Cross Street and Tanter Street (then called The Butts) were cut out and the area was marked as land for building. Later, Cross Street became **Old Cross Street** and part of it was named **Vauxhall Street**; whilst because of its bad reputation **Tanter Street** was restyled **Ryder Street** at the time of the Corporation Street Improvement Scheme. This name arose from the Bishop Ryder Memorial Church in Gem Street, commemorating Henry Ryder a former Bishop of Lichfield.

D

Dale End

This is one of the oldest street names in the city, for in 1454 William Bermyngham knight and lord of Birmingham granted to John Bradewell of Birmingham one croft of land in Dale End. A croft was an enclosed piece of land and usually was cultivated. Then in 1485, John Lenche of Byrmyngham granted one burgage in Dale End to John Trayford of Byrmyngham and Mergerie his wife. Because a burgage was a standard house plot this would seem to show that the settled part of Birmingham had begun to stretch up from Saint Martin's. Subsequently, Dale End barres was noted in the 1553 Survey of Birmingham (see Bull Street). A continuation of High Street, Dale End was at the end of a dale and on the road to Coleshill – and later it led into Coleshill Street itself.

Part of Dale End in 1961, and soon to be demolished. Thanks to the *Birmingham Evening Mail*.

Dalton Street

Named after John Dalton, a chemist and member of the Society of Friends from Cumbria, Dalton Street replaced **London Prentice Street** and part of **Silver Street** in 1882. Supposedly called after an apprentice from London who set up business in the locality, London Prentice Street was mentioned in an advertisement from 1769. Seven years later in Birmingham's first directory it is given both as London-'prentice-street and London Apprentice-street. Narrow and short, it came to be looked down upon as one of the worst slums in the Birmingham and in *Showell's Dictionary* it was declared to be a 'nasty, dirty, stinking thoroughfare'.

The Corporation Street Redevelopment Scheme (see Corporation Street) led to the clearance of the properties in London Prentice Street and to the changing of its name in 1882. In reality, as with The Gullett and other streets stalked by poverty, London Prentice Street was the home of the poor and from the 1820s it was inhabited mostly by Irish Brummies from the west of Ireland. One of them was John Hannon. In 1837, Thomas Finigan, an Irish missionary seeking to convert Catholics into Protestants, wrote of Hannon's plight. For eighteen months he had been afflicted by sickness occasioned by overworking himself and was confined to his bed. He and his wife were supported by their two daughters aged fourteen and thirteen who were pin headers, 'but for the last four or five weeks they got nothing to earn – in consequence of the bad state of the trade'. The disappearance of London Prentice Street also led to the extinction of **Rope Walk**, renamed **Dalton Place** in 1896.

Daniels Road, Little Bromwich

A schoolmaster from Gloucestershire, Francis William Daniels came to Birmingham as district manager of the Sceptre Life Association. He had a major impact upon the city and wrote a booklet explaining the objects and advantages of the Birmingham Mutual Sick Benefit and Old Age Society (1893), and also the *Explanatory Book of the Ideal Benefit Society and the Birmingham Mutual Bank, Limited* (1907). The first general manager of the Ideal Benefit Society, Daniels oversaw the development of the Ideal Benefit Estate in Little Bromwich where there is a Daniels Road, cut in 1913, and **Finnemore Road**, named after an early chairman of the society. The Ideal Benefit was also responsible for the Cherry Orchard Estate Handsworth Wood, where **Ebley Road** brings to mind the village near Stroud from which Daniels came; whilst **Inverclyde Road** and **Cooper Road** are named after officials of the society.

Dawberry Fields Road, Stirchley

Dawberry Fields Farm house was at the junction of Dawberry Fields Road and Harton Way. It was knocked down after the Second World War. The name is also brought to mind in **Dawberry Road**.

Dawson Road, Handsworth

This road would seem to be named after George Dawson, the great preacher and advocate of the Civic Gospel who so influenced Joseph Chamberlain and other politicians with his call for men of wealth to enter public life and act for the well being of the community at large. Formerly **Bridle Road**, it was renamed Dawson Road in 1879, three years after the death of Dawson and at a time when a public subscription was raising funds for a statue of him. Born in London, Dawson came to Birmingham in 1844 aged 23 to take charge of the Mount Zion chapel. Markedly independent of mind, Dawson soon moved on to his own Church of the Saviour in Edward Street, later the 'Lyric' picture house. Here worshippers of all faiths were pulled in by the charisma of this extraordinary preacher.

Of middle height, robust and broad set, Dawson's black hair cascaded down over his ears and his forehead, and a thick beard flowed over his neck and to the top of his chest. Dressed in a long velvet coat that stretched to his knees and a colourful necktie, he was one of the most powerful speakers of the age. He declared that Jesus had not died for man but lived for him. He exhorted his listeners to follow Our Lord's example and not think of what should not be done but of what more could be done. He chastised those who did not live their beliefs daily and who felt that they need only act as Christians on a Sunday. He urged each citizen to strive 'to clothe the naked, to feed the hungry, and to instruct the ignorant'. And he proclaimed that 'a great town is a solemn organism through which should flow, and in which should be shaped, all the highest, loftiest and truest ends of man's intellectual and moral nature'.

Dawson's preaching and passion inspired Joseph Chamberlain and others to make this Civic Gospel reality and the reforms carried out by Chamberlain (see Chamberlain Square) owed much to George Dawson. He died unexpectedly in 1876, just as Chamberlain's municipal socialism was beginning to improve the lives of all Brummies. Vice president of the Birmingham Freehold Land Society (see Franchise Street), Dawson was honoured by the society in the development of their Small Heath Estate by the naming of **Dawson Street**. Coming off Muntz Street and opposite Kenelm Road, it disappeared in the 1960s and now is playing fields. **Watford Road**, Cotteridge recalls George Dawson's home that was on the corner of the Pershore Road South and Middleton Hall Road, where he died.

Deakin Road, Erdington

Deakin Road in Erdington is named after a prominent member of the Erdington Urban District Council, the local government authority until the district became part of Birmingham in 1911. **Deykin Road**, Witton, formed in 1904, may be a misspelling of James Deakin, one of the main owners of land in Witton. **Deakins Road**, Hay Mills and Yardley recalls Deakin's Farm that was near to the Hob Moor Ford of the River Cole on the Yardley side.

Dean Street, City

Going uphill from Sherlock Street, across Bromsgove Street and into **Upper Dean Street**, in the 1950s Dean Street was distinguished by the wheelwright's of F. Parr, which had five wheels hanging up outside his shop. Joe McKenna feels that the street recalls Dr Thomas Sherlock, who was Dean of Chichester and later Bishop of Bangor and Bishop of London (see Gooch Street). However, in *Showell's Dictionary* it is stated that John a' Dean's Hole was a little brook which took water from the moat which once surrounded the old manor house and which flowed into the River Rea at Floodgate Street(see Moat Lane). According to an old story, a John Dean drowned in this brook some time during the reign of King Henry VIII, hence the later Dean Street. The street had appeared by the time of Kempson's Map of 1810. Since the oppening of the new Bull Ring Shopping Centre in September 2003, Upper Dean Street has become one of the busiest bus lanes in Birmingham.

Derby Street, Bordesley

An abstract of title relating to the years 1809-17 mentions the heiresses of Thomas Derby and houses in Moland Street. Running between Montague Street and Great Barr Street, Derby Street may take its name from this family, but it is more likely that it relates to the Birmingham and Derby Junction Railway which opened in 1839 with a terminus nearby to Derby Street in Lawley Street.

Deritend High Street

Although it belonged for hundreds of years to the parish of Aston, Deritend has been bound inextricably to Birmingham from the beginnings of the market in 1166. Indeed, old documents always mention Deritend as part of the lordship of Birmingham and do not mention Aston. It is likely that Deritend's development came before that of Digbeth. Described in the late fourteenth century as a manor in its own right, it may have emerged as market street formed by its lord in an attempt to gain trade and income from the successful Birmingham. If this is the case, the presence of a rival led the de Berminghams to acquire Deritend by 1270 at least. In effect, Deritend then became part of the borough of Birmingham.

Deritend High Street has the distinction of the first of Birmingham's streets to be described. In 1538 John Leland visited the town, coming down Camp Hill through 'as pretty a street or ever I entrd'. This was Deritend High Street, or 'Dirtey' as Leland called it.

> In it dwell smithes and cutlers, and there is a brooke that divideth this street from Birmingham, and is an Hamlett, or member belonginge to the Parish therebye (Aston).
>
> There is at the end of Dirtey a proper chappell (St John's) and mansion house of tymber (the 'Old Crown' pub), hard on the ripe (bank), as the brooke runneth downe; and as I went through the ford by the bridge, the water ran

downe on the right hande (later Floodgate Street) and a few miles lower goeth into Tame, ripa dextra (by the right bank).

Given as Darytend in a Copy of Chantry Lands Unsold in 1562, the name is problematical. Joe McKenna believes that the 'der' is derived from the Welsh 'dwr' meaning water, whilst the rest of the name is from 'yet-end' – signifying gate end. Thus it was the water gate end because of its proximity to the River Rea. It seems unlikely that this interpretation is correct. There are only a handful of names within modern Birmingham which may be derived from the British who lived here before the Anglo-Saxons. In these circumstances, the best explanation for Deritend is that of Joseph Toulmin Smith. He was a nineteenth-century expert on Birmingham and the 'Old Crown', Deritend belonged to his family. In his opinion Deritend is from 'der-yat-end' and means the deer gate end. This name arose from the deer park which had been on the north side of Bradford Street by Alcester Street. Thus Deritend was the end of Birmingham near the deer gate, 'that is, near to the common way into the woodlands of Aston'. William Hamper, another nineteenth- century researcher of Birmingham, disagreed and felt that Deritend meant the Rea gate end. Toulmin Smith's case seems the stronger.

This atmospheric photo from the 1930s shows the 'Golden Lion' inn and the church of Saint John the Baptist on High Street, Deritend. After the Second World War, the 'Golden Lion' was moved to Cannon Hill Park, whilst the church and other buildings were knocked down for road widening. Thanks to Mr H. C. Lacey.

Today the historic and ongoing importance of Deritend High Street is reflected in the survival of the 'Old Crown', the 'mansion house of tymber' mentioned by Leland and by a collection of long-established buildings running up from the pub towards Bordesley High Street. Going the other way, towards Digbeth, the Custard Factory arts complex is a fine example of how an enterprising figure can regenerate a redundant factory – the former Bird's Custard works. The other side of Deritend High Street was knocked down for road widening in the 1950s. This scheme led to the clearance of many old buildings, including Saint John's Church, the 'proper chappell' noted by Leland.

Devil's Hollow Tooth Yard

This mysteriously named yard was a short and narrow passage that emerged in the 1600s and went from Bull Street to the Horse Close – which lay alongside where Saint Philip's Church would be built. In later years it ran alongside Grey's department store and into Colmore Row. It survived until the 1950s.

Digbeth

Running downhill from the Bull Ring and Park Street to the River Rea, Digbeth is part of Birminghamn's oldest and most important street line. When Brum's market opened in 1166 it was placed alongside the road which ran from Coventry to Wolverhampton. As the town grew, sections of this road were given different names. Beginning with High Street Bordesley, it went on as High Street Deritend, Digbeth, Bull Ring, High Street Birmingham, Bull Street, Snow Hill, Constitution Hill, Great Hampton Street and Hockley Hill. Of them all, Digbeth and Deritend are the street names which are most rooted in the past.

Birmingham's first historian was William Hutton and according to him 'Dygbeth' meant Ducks Bath, recalling the pools where these birds were kept. Another account states that the Ducks Bath was a spring. Interestingly a stretch of Digbeth was once known as **Well Street** and there is still a **Well Lane** nearby. In fact, for many years various outlets in Digbeth supplied the water for many Brummies and in the mid-1800s Coffee and Sons advertised their soda water as 'manufactured from their celebrated Digbeth Spring'.

A less colourful but more likely explanation for the name is that Digbeth is derived from the Anglo-Saxon words 'dic poeth,' indicating the dyke's path. In 1482-3 a deed stated that John Lench of Deritend, master of the Guild of Holy Cross, with the unanimous assent of the brothers and sisters of the guild, leased to William Wyot a tanner of Brum a parcel of land 'lying jux le cawsy' – next to the causeway. In a lecture reported in the *Evening Despatch* in 1913, W.H. Foxall explained how this causeway may have come about. In Anglo-Saxon times the River Rea was wider and deeper than it is now. As a result it flooded more, so causing the Lake Meadow below Park Street. This flooding was made worse by little brooks such as **Hersum's Dyche**

Relaying the tram track in Digbeth in 1940. The Digbeth Institute is on the right, with the dome above it, and Digbeth Police Station is above that.

which flowed down from the fields on Bennett's Hill. Sometime in the Middle Ages, the Rea was diverted to provide power for Birmingham's mill. This caused two branches of the river. To achieve this deviation it was necessary to bank up the new course, making a dike. Then it was essential to build a pathway to the old stream which would clear the low wet land between the two branches of the river.

Whatever its origins the importance of Digbeth cannot be understated and it led to the oldest roads in Brum. It was lined with houses at a later date than the Bull Ring area, but it became the fulcrum of early Birmingham. For many years it boasted the slitting mill of Sampson Lloyd, a co-founder of the banking company, and it was the busiest thoroughfare in the town – so much so that in 1761 it was declared 'very dangerous to travel through, on horseback or otherwise'. The great number of travellers had plenty of pubs to choose from. There was the 'White Hart', the 'Talbot', the 'Red Lion' and the country-style 'White Lion' just down from Saint Martin's. The rural feel of Digbeth was made more noticeable by the adjoining fields and a number of large houses with walled gardens. Their owners were manufacturers and tradesmen, but gradually they moved up the slope to the fresher air and dryer land of Bennett's Hill and the High Town, especially after the forming of Old Square early in the eighteenth century.

With the expansion of Birmingham, by the earlyt nineteenth century Digbeth was the focal point of a major working-class neighbourhood and it soon came to have a number of major landmarks. There was the 'Royal George' pub on the corner of Park Street with the model of a ship on its walls and an eye-catching police station with a Dutch looking clock tower. Then, of course, there was the Digbeth Institute, built on a site previously occupied by the Birmingham Battery; the premises of Avery's the scale makers; and the bus garages. In 1954 a road-widening scheme swept away the west side of Digbeth and in the subsequent decade, most of the houses to the east were knocked down and their folk moved to distant parts of Brum.

Digby Walk, Garretts Green

The Digbys held lands in Castle Bromwich, hence **Digby Crescent** in Water Orton, Sheldon, to which Garretts Green belonged, and elsewhere in north Warwickshire, and from the early eighteenth century they lived at Meriden Hall. When Sir Lister Holte (see Holte Road) died without isue in 1770, he left his lands to his brother Charles and afterwards successively to the nephews of his first wife – Heneage Legge and Lewis Bagot, Bishop of Saint Asaph. If their issue failed the properties were to go to Wriothesley Digby and if his issue failed, then the estates were to go to Charles Holte's daughter. Surprisingly given all the caveats, Mary Holte became the heir to the lands. However, her husband Abraham Bracebridge mortgaged his wife's inheritance and because of bad business deals, the lands reverted to the Legges and the Digbys. When he developed Gosta Green, Heneage Legge named **Digby Street** after his co-beneficiary.

A co-op milk float in Monica Road in 1956. Thanks to John Roberts.

In 1802 a grant was made both by Heneage Legge to George Birch and by the Reverend Noel Digby to Richard Congreve in trust of tithes of Witton. Then after Wriothesley Digby died an Act of Parliament was passed in 1839 which enabled Jane Mills to grant building and repairing leases of estates in Aston devised by the will of Wriothesly Digby. The Digbys share of the Holte lands was to the north of the Coventry Road in Small Heath (then in the parish of Aston). It extended from Grange Road to the River Cole and included Hey Barnes Farm – hence **Heybarnes Road**. Part of this farm was built upon between 1895-1915, with the remainder following in the 1920s after the farm house was demolished. It stood on the present **Ravensdale Road**.

The research of Vivian Bird has emphasised the number of road names in Small Heath which derive from the Digbys. **Kenelm Road** recalls Sir Kenelm Digby, a philospher, poet and taveller. It is said that he married Venetia Stanley, hence **Venetia Road**, who was a beauty of the court of James I. Keen to keep her exquisite complexion, Sir Kenelm gave her viper's wine which killed her. I have been unable to verify this. However, Sir Kenelm did lead a naval expedition in 1628 that defeated a French and Venetian force in the Mediterranean and it may be that Venetia Road recalls this victory over the Venetians.

Somerville Road and **Hugh Road** are called after the Honourable Hugh Somerville, the 18th Lord Somerville, whose daughter married into the Digbys in 1775; whilst **Charles Road** and **Dora Road** bring to mind Charles Wriothesley

Digby who married Dora Adelaide Featherstonehaugh-Frampton in 1881. **Monica Road** relates to another member of the family and **Heather Road** commemorates the favourite horse of one the daughters of the Digbys. On the former Garrison Farm Estate, **Tilton Road** (**Kelynge Street** until 1897) is called after Tilton-on-the-Hill in Leicestershire, where the Digbys originated. **Greenaway Street** and **Cattell Street** remember business associates of the Digbys – and on the former Hey Barnes estate so do a number of other roads. Amongst them are **Floyer Road, Bankes Road** (named after an army captain and formed in 1894) and **Mansell Road** – recalling Colonel Mansell, a trustee of the Digby Estate. **Swanage Road** bears the name of the Dorset seat of the Digbys; whilst also connected with the family is **Cattell Road**. Formerly this was **China Temple Field**, around 1820 a place for amusements that had a Chinese pagoda. The field is brought to mind in **Templefield Street**.

The Digbys themselves came to prominence at the Battle of Bosworth in 1485 when six brothers supported Henry Tudor against Richard III. With Henry's victory and accession as Henry VII, the Digbys' power waxed, especially that of the youngest son Simon, who came into possession of Coleshill in 1496 and from where they expanded their interests in Warwickshire.

Dixon Road, Small Heath

In the 1870s, Major General Dixon occupied a large house on the Coventry Road close to the corner with Tennyson Rd. The building itself belonged to the wealthy Rylands (see Ryland Street), but it seems more likely that Dixon Road is named after George Dixon, a Yorkshireman who became a prominent figure in nineteenth-century Birmingham. He came to the town when he was aged eighteen, and within six years had become a partner in Rabone Brothers, the rule makers of Hockley. In 1863 he was elected a councillor and he was the justice of the peace who read the riot act as mayor during the Murphy Riots of 1867. These arose from the vehemently anti-Catholic preachings of a Protestant rabble rouser called William Murphy and they led to severe conflict between the English and Irish in Birmingham, during which the Irish Quarter in Park Street was sacked.

Despite his newness to the council, Dixon was elected mayor in 1866 and as such presided over a conference on national education which led to the forming of the National Education League at his home (see also Chamberlain Square). He was passionately concerned with opening up education to people of all classes and for many years he was chairman of the Birmingham School Board. This was set up following the Education Act of 1870 which enabled elected boards to levy a rate and build schools in their area. His contribution in the educational sphere later led to the naming of George Dixon School.

Dixon was elected to Parliament as one of Birmingham's two Liberal MPs in 1867. The following year the number of MPs in the town was increased to three and in the general election, Dixon was returned at the of the poll. He remained an MP until 1876 and was drawn back into national politics when Joseph Chamberlain broke with the Liberals in 1885, over his opposition to the granting of Home Rule to Ireland, and set up the Liberal Unionist Party. Dixon joined the new grouping. The election of that year was the first in which the Parliamentary Borough of Birmingham had been split into seven divisions and Dixon was elected for Edgbaston. He stayed in his post until 1897. Asa Briggs has declared that Dixon's record of public service was 'as remarkable as that of any many who has ever worked for the city'. In 1898, Dixon was made a freeman of the city 'in grateful acknowledgment of his eminent public servives and in recognition of his untiring energy and devotion in the interests of Elementary Education'.

The Dingle, Selly Oak and The Dingles, Hall Green

In Middle English, the word dingle meant hollow. The Dingles in Yardley Wood runs alongside the River Cole and thus is in a hollow, whilst The Dingle in Selly Oak does lead downhill. This latter public driveway emerged in the mid-1800s as a connection between the Birmingham to Worcester Canal, and a wharf thereon, and the Bristol Road. In his *The Story of Selly Oak*, Francis W. Leonard dispels optimistic visions of The Dingle when he wrote, 'The Dingle has a pretty name, but it was never a very pretty place. On the left, going down The Dingle, were six houses, and at the end, facing the canal was an old Inn called the "Boat Inn" kept by a Mr Kinchin.' By the side of The Dingle was a private road leading to Sturge's Chemical Works (see Elliott Road).

The Dingle, Yardley Wood

Watering the horse in the River Cole at the Dingles, Yardley Wood in the late 1800s.

Dr Johnson Passage

Going from the top of Bull Street to The Square (Old Square), the passage refers to Dr Samuel Johnson, the compiler of dictionaries, critic and poet. Born and raised in Lichfield, his mother hailed from Kings Norton and he came to Birmingham when he was ten to visit his uncle. He was not impressed by his relative whom he called 'a very mean and vulgar man, drunk every night, but drunk with very little drink, very peevish, very proud, very ostentatious, but, luckily, not rich'. It is also likely that Johnson made trips with his father, who sold books in Birmingham's market. Later he stayed for six months with his friend, Edmund Hector, who had moved from Lichfield in about 1731 to lodge with Thomas Warren in The Square in Birmingham. Johnson spent much of his time in bed, dictating his first book to Hector. Then, the writer moved to accommodation in Bull Street, meeting the Widow Porter, whom he married. Over the next few years he flitted between Birmingham and Lichfield before he headed to London – although he did make other visits to Brum to see Hector and other friends. Dr Johnson Passage appeared in 1883, and although now gone the man of letters is recalled in Dr Johnson House in Bull Street.

Dog Yard, Bull Ring

Coming off the lower part of Spiceal Street, this took its name from the 'Talbot' inn, also known as the 'Dog' inn. Apparent by the early eighteenth century, it was cleared in the 1870s.

Dogpool Lane, Ten Acres

This may take its name from a pool where docks or water lilies grew, and it is interesting to note that there was a **Dogge Lane** mentioned near to the present Hazelwood Road in 1580. Certainly there is a pool in the vicinity, just to the west of the River Rea and close to where the river is joined by the Griffin's Brook. Dogpool Mill was mentioned in 1800 and in the twentieth century it was owned by C. Clifford and Sons, metal rollers and tube makers.

Dolphin Lane, Acock's Green

Known as **Green Lane** until the early 1900s, this became Dolphin Lane because of the Dolphin pub which stood on the Warwick Road and the site of which now is a supermarket. The pub itself recalls the Dolphin family who moved from Solihull to Swanshurst Farm, on the borders of Moseley and Billesley. Mentioned first in 1221, Swanshurst means the small wood (hurst) of a peasant or herdsman (swan) or else a wooded hill where swans gathered. Obviously, **Swanshurst Lane** brings to mind the farm. The Dolphins are noted from the late 1300s and from 1495 they are definitely associated with Swanshurst Farm. They remained there until 1854 when John Dolphin died a bachelor. A branch of the Dolphins later settled in Bordesley. One of the earliest references to this family dates to 1655 when land and premises in this district was settled by Edward Dolphin upon his wife, Elizabeth, and his son, Edmund. In 1740 an Edward Dolphin is given as an attorney, and some of the male members of the family practiced as lawyers in Birmingham into the nineteenth century.

Drews Lane, Washwood Heath

Known formerly as **Mill Lane**, it became Drews Lane in 1897, bringing to mind John Drew, one of the tenants of Ward End Mill. The mill lay on the Wash Brook, north of Ward End Hall, in Little Bromwich and was mentioned first in 1425. The mill has been filled in and forms part of **Ingleton Road**, which runs from Drews Lane to Saint Margaret's Road, Ward End. Later famed for the Wolseley Motor Works, Drews Lane is now well known for the production of LDV vans.

The Ward End Flour Mill, Drews Lane in the early twentieth century.

Druids Lane, Druids Heath

Unfortunately for local stories which tells of druids in the area, Druid's Heath is a corruption of Drew's Heath, taking its name from a family which farmed locally until the 1840s. However, when the council laid out the Druid's Heath Estate after the Second World War the belief in ancient tales led to the naming of roads with connections with Stonehenge in Wiltshire. Amongst them are **Stonehenge Road** and **Netheravon Close**.

Duddeston Mill Road, Duddeston

Meaning the farmstead of Dudda, Duddeston is one of the oldest place names in Birmingham and is mentioned as Duddestone in a deed from the reign of King Edgar in 963. It is likely that the Duddeston Mill itself was built about 1530 as there was a mill field in Duddeston by 1531. Both the buildings and the mill pool lay on the west bank of the River Rea above Duddeston Mill Road. In the 1570s 'three new water corn mills in Duddeston' were built in an agreement between Edward Holte of Duddeston and Edward Arden, who owned Saltley Mill (on the east side of the Rea and above Saltley Bridge). By 1756, when it was visited by William Hutton, Duddeston Mill was a mill for rolling metal and probably was leased by the Farmer family of ironmongers. In the early nineteenth century the mill reverted to agricultural uses, especially for corn, but soon after 1865 the mill pool was drained. At the same time, the Great Moor, which had lain between the mill leat (the ditch which took the water to the mill wheel) became a railway goods yard. The buildings later were used as a saw mill.

David Rice informs me that lying off Duddeston Mill Road were a number of back-to-back yards that were interconnected to each other through a number of entries and double knacks (a yard with two entries). This maze of buildings and terraces was known as the **Bum's Puzzle** because the bummers, baliffs, could not find their way around when looking to take possession of goods from someone who was in rent arrears. There was also a Bum's Puzzle in Ladywood. (For **Duddeston Row** see Bartholomew Street).

B. Ingram's is partially boarded up and awaiting demolition on the corner of Duddeston Mill Road, on the right, and Great Francis Street in the early 1950s.

DUDLEY ROAD, BIRMINGHAM

The Dudley Road in the 1930s.

Dudley Road, Winson Green and Rotton Park

A lane to Dudley was noted in 1565, and in 1727 the road to Dudley was described as in great use for the carriage of iron goods, coal and lime. Sixty years later, Hutton damned it as 'despicable beyond description'. This statement was made twenty-seven years after the Dudley, Birmingham and Wolverhampton Turnpike had been set up. By the 1870s, this company had dispapeared and the Dudley Road in Birmingham was the responsibility of the corporation.

Dudley Street, City

There is some debate about this name. Mike Hodder, Birmingham City Archaeologist believes that it was the beginning of the route to Dudley. This was an important road as the manor of Birmingham belonged to the lords of Dudley. Others argue that name does not relate to the town of Dudley, instead it is a corruption of the word Dodwalles or Dudwalls. Recorded in a document of 1532, the Dodwalles was a pasture of eighty acres in the vicinity of the later Dudley Street. The walles element of the name may mean either wall or bank, from the Old English weall, or spring or stream; whilst Dod might from the Old English man's name, Dudda. Dudley Street was originally Dudwall Lane, as is indicated in the Survey of Birmingham in 1553, but by the time of Westley's map of 1731 it is given as Dudley Street. In the same year, a lease from John Ashwell and John Kent to Joseph Stockley also mentioned Dudley Street and Peck Lane. Dudley Street runs from the junction of Edgbaston Street and Smallbrook Street up to Pinfold Street.

Looking up from Pershore Street, Dudley Street is on the left and Worcester is running up hill.

Dyott Road, Moseley

In the early 1800s, a Joseph Dyott owned extensive property in the Wake Green district of Moseley.

E

Easy Row

Easy Row, formerly **Baskerville Street**, once ran from Cambridge Street to Suffolk Street. A short street on the west of town, it took its name from Easy Hill – the slopes of which were gentle or 'easy.' Despite the developments in the neighbourhood in the late 1700s and early 1800s, Easy Row itself retained a rural feel. This was because of several large elm trees in which rooks built nests and which stood on the corner of Edmund Street. They were cut down in 1847, having become skeletons through pollution.

By now Easy Row had become a street of importance. In particular it boasted a magnificent public house 'The Woodman'. Standing three floors high, it was made eye-catching by ornate pillars, attractive windows and two grand lamps. But the most impressive features of all were the figures of a woodman and his dog, set in a niche halfway up the building. In the 1850s the gaffer was Jem Onions and his pub was the rendezvous of leading politicians who discussed the council's business while they drank their ale and puffed on their long clay pipes.

In 1891 'The Woodman' was refurbished and decorated with magnificent tile panels which depicted scenes from Brum's history. There was one of the Battle of Birmingham in 1643, when Prince Rupert and his Royalists attacked our town; and

Fgeorge arthur road in 1903. These fine buildings were swept away in the mid-1960s as part of the building of the Inner Ring Road.

another of the Town Hall as it was seen from the bottom of Hill Street. Disgracefully the 'Woodman' was destroyed in 1965 when the cutting of the Inner Ring Road led to the disappearance of Easy Row itself. Little is left to remind us of the street's presence, apart from a plaque close to the underpass leading to the Central Library.

Edgbaston Street

This is one of the oldest street names in Birmingham and is noted in 1449 when Roger Cutte of Erdyngton granted to John Kockes of Birmingham and Julianne his wife, one burgage and butcher's shop and land in Edgbaston Strete. A burgage was a standard house plot held by yearly rent from the lord of the manor originally. This would suggest that traders were gathered about Saint Martin's in the historic neighbourhood of the Bull Ring. Edgbaston Street continues to be of major importance and along it is now sited a new Market Hall and Rag Market as well as the outdoor traders of the Bull Ring. The word Edgbaston itself is of Anglo-Saxon origin and means the farmstead ('tun') of a man called Ecgbald. It has given its name to **Edgbaston Road**, Balsall Heath and Moseley, and **Edgbaston Park Road**, Edgbaston called **Hall Hill Road** and **Park Road** until 1882.

Firefighters in Edgbaston Street on 10 April 1940, after a heavy night of bombing on Birmingham. Saint Martin's Church is on the right of the photograph. Thanks to the *Birmingham Evening Mail*.

Edward Road, Balsall Heath

The Reverend Vincent Edwardes and his wife Jane Mary are brought to mind in Edward Road (**Edwardes Street** until 1899), **Vincent Street**, **Vincent Parade**, **Vincent Crescent** and **Mary Street**, Balsall Heath. The land through which these streets was cut was developed after an Act of Parliament of 1833 allowed the sale of building lots and other property following the death of the Reverend. Development was gradual and as late as 1850 blackberry canes and nutbushes were growing locally by the Pike Pool on the River Rea.

Edward Road, Balsall Heath in 1957.

Egghill Lane, Northfield

An Egghill Cottage is shown on the Kings Norton Map in 1899. It may take its name from the Anglo-Saxon Ecca's or Ecga's hill

Elan Road, Northfield

For much of the nineteenth century, drinking water in Birmingham was provided by private companies that sold it from water butts taken around the streets in wagons. Such water was brackish and unsavoury, as was the water drawn from many of the numerous wells in the town. These were polluted by manufactories and by the seepage of human and animal excreta that resulted from the lack of an effective refuse system. The same problem affected water taken from streams. There was also a Birmingham Waterworks Company, a private concern set up in 1826 by an act of Parliament. It drew water from the River Tame and did provide a constant supply to some parts of the town, although in 1849 this was deemed insufficient and expensive.

Given the problems with drinking water it is not surprising that diseases were so widespread and that beer drinking was so popular, as brewers advertised that they used pure water. It fell to the dynamic Joseph Chamberlain to lead a campaign to privatise the waterworks company, achieved by legislation in 1875. The supply of fresh water was extended considerably from sources around Birmingham but it was admitted that the demand was too high for it be met locally. Accordingly in 1892 an act of Parliament was obtained to provide a supply of water from Wales and construct the Elan Valley scheme, near to Rhayader in mid-Wales, hence **Rhayader Road**, Northfield. The Elan Valley Dam was opened in 1904 at a cost of £6 million and was built by hand. Within a year the whole of Birmingham was receiving supplies of fresh water from Wales. By 1939, the city was consuming 28 million gallons of water daily and a third pipe was laid from Elan Valley to Birmingham. As demand continued to grow, work began on a fourth pipe in 1949 and another dam was opened at Clearwen in 1952, leading to **Claerwan Road**, Northfield.

The Elan Valley scheme was a remarkable feat of engineering, as were the pipes which feed the city with 80 million gallons a day by way of gravity feed. It takes two and half days for the water to reach Frankley Reservoir after it has left Elan Valley. Part of **Tessal Lane** was renamed Elan Road in1928 to honour the achievement of the Corporation. It lies near to Northfield Reservoir. Rhayader Road and Claerwen Road are near to the water works, filter beds and reservoir at Frankley.

Electric Avenue, Witton

Hallmore Road until 1902, this brings to mind the great works of the General Electric Company. Although not arising in Birmingham, the GEC set up a branch locally in 1896. Three years later it acquired land in Witton. By 1932 it was employing 10,000 people. The factory has now gone.

Elkington Street, Aston

Known as **Blews Street** until 1881, rather than referring to the famed manufacturing Elkingtons of the Jewellery Quarter, this may recall a George Elkington who was house surgeon for the Aston Union. This was a workhouse union which had followed on from the Poor Law Amendment Act of 1834. There unions were responsible for relieving the poor, giving them help. This could be done outdoors, by giving tokens for bread and coal to applicants living in their own homes; or indoors in the workhouse. Because the Act sought to punish the poor for their poverty and to stop them from asking for help from 'the parish', strenuous efforts were made to stop outdoor relief. At the same time, the poor were deterred for asking for help in the workhouse because of prison-like conditions whereby 'inmates' had to wear uniforms, do hard and physical work and be split up from their partners and children. Over time, many unions realised that those applying for help were the aged, infirm, forlorn, abandoned, mentally ill and physically disabled and so began to develop social service facilities such as infirmaries.

Eliot Street, Nechells

Connecting Long Acre and Nechells Park Road, Eliot Street was called **Hutton Street** until 1897 and it may relate to the Reverend W. Eliot, a vicar of Aston Parish Church and a prominent member of the Aston School Board. Although part of Birmingham from 1838, Nechells remained in Aston for schooling purposes. Like Poor Law Unions, School Boards were run by committees elected by property owners and were entitled to levy rates on property owners. Out of the school rate, new board schools could be built. Throughout the country, school boards were riven in two over the nature of religious teaching, between Non-Conformists on the one side and Catholics and Anglicans on the other. The Reverend Eliot was a controversial character who pressed for Bible teaching in Aston Board schools as opposed to the Bible reading without note or comment favoured by the Non-Conformists. The Church Party in Aston was victorious in the elections of 1881 and the Reverend Eliot was a chairman of the board.

Ellis Street, City

It is thought that this is named after a Shropshire family who owned land locally. It was laid out by 1792 and from the mid-1800s it became one of Birmingham's two small Jewish Quarters. The other was in Hurst Street/Inge Street. (See Blucher Street and Inge Street).

Elliott Rd, Selly Oak

Started in 1793, Elliot's Patent Sheathing and Metal Company moved to Selly Oak in 1853, taking over Albright and Sturge's chemical works site on the Birmingham to Worcester Canal. Elliott Road was known first as **Commercial Road**. Nearby **Katie Road**, **Winnie Road** and **Lottie Road** are called after the daughters of Henry Elliott. He built the British Workman's Hall as a club, library, reading room and concert venue for the growing population of Selly Oak, and was later involved in providing an evening technical school for his workers. Elliott's was taken over by Kynoch's, soon to become I.C.I. Metals in 1928.

Erdington Hall Road

Probably meaning the settlement of a man called Earda, Erdington is given as Hardintone in the Domesday Book of 1086. It had become Erdintone by 1260 and Erdyngtone by 1461. In this year the name was also given as Yerdington and on a map of Warwickshire dated 1610 the area is shown as Yenton. Indeed, as late as the 1830s Eliezer Edwards explained that Erdington was 'then universally called Yarnton'. Erdington Hall itself was the home of the de Erdington family, which took its name from the manor. A fortified manor house with a chapel and double moat, Erdington Hall was held by the de Erdingtons for around 300 years from the mid-twelfth century. Rebuilt a number of times, it was knocked down to make way for the Tyburn Road just before the First World War. It stood close to the 'Navigation Inn' on the way to Salford Bridge.

Essington Street, Ladywood

The 1873 Return of Onwer's Land for Warwickshire gives a W.W. Essington of Aston as owning 163 acres. He may be recalled in Essington Street.

Este Road, Yardley

The Est or Este family appeared in Yardley from the early fifteenth century. As Victor Skipp's meticulous research reveals they were amongst a number of families that had a deep effect upon the parish. Amongst the others were the Dolphins (see Dolphin Road), the Flavells (see Flavell Road), and the Greswolde's (see Greswolde Road). The Est presence was founded by Thomas. He was a noteworthy person – a governor of Kenilworth Castle, a gentleman of the bedchamber to Henry V and Henry VI, and a distinguished soldier in the wars against the French. Indeed, he fought at the Battle of Agincourt. He married Marion, the daughter of William Del Hay in 1423 and so acquired Hay Hall, which is present still in Redfern Road, Tyseley and led to the naming of **Hay Hall Road**. The central part of the house has an arch-braced collar-beam roof truss and could represent an open hall of the fourteenth or fifteenth centuries. Other feautures indicate addition s from the Tudor period and later.

Thomas and his wife are shown in Saint Edburga's Church in the top of an incised alabaster tomb chest. He has short hair and pointed shoes, whilst his wife is at prayer and wears a heart-shaped head-dress. When their descendant, Edward Este died a bachelor in 1703, Hay Hall and its lands passed through various owners. The estate itself was sold in 1763. It consisted of nearly 200 acres bordering the 'very good trout stream' of the River Cole, and also had a mill. This had been recorded first in 1495 when it was spelled as Hayemill.

Eyre Street, Brookfields

Like the nearby Coralie Street and Rosalie Street, Eyre Street had a pronunciation peculiar to Brummies. Denis G. Rathbone moved there when he was six and stresses that it was given as Eye-er Street by locals.

Lost Streets

Street	Location	Clearance Date
Coach Yard		1884
Cotton Row	off Fazeley Street	1884
Cotton Street	off Fazeley Street	1884
Engine Street	off New Canal Street	1886
Forge Street	off Mill Street, Aston Road	1886

Renamed Streets

Present Name	Former Name
Adams Street, Duddeston	Brewery Street (changed 1880) and Clarkson Street (changed 1905)
Albany Road, Harborne	Green Road (changed 1883)
Alfred Street, Hockley	Warstone Parade East (1873)
Arden Road, Acocks Green	Quality Lane (changed 1897)
Ashwin Road, Handsworth	Slade Road (renamed 1907)
Athole Street, Highgate	Wharf Street (changed before 1879)
Barwell Road, Garrison Lane	Couchman Road (changed 1879)
Belchers Lane, Stechford	Mills Lane (changed 1897)
Belgrave Road, Balsall Heath and Highgate	Belgrave Street (changed 1898)
Bevington Road, Aston	Upper Sutton Street, part of (changed 1878)
Broad Meadow Lane, Kings Heath	Broad Meadow Road (mentioned 1774)
Bromley Street, Deritend	Penn Street (changed 1898)
Broughton Road, Handsworth	Hall Roads (changed 1901)
Chandos Road, Highgate	Mount Pleasant
Clonmel Road, Stirchley	Ascot Road (changed 1902)
Clyde Street, Bordesley	Mount Street (changed 1887)
Couchman Road, Alum Rock	Castle Street
Cranby Street, Saltley	William Street (changed 1898)
Cromer Road, Balsall Heath	Priory Road (changed 1897)

Cuckoo Road, Nechells	Cuckoo Lane (changed 1870)
Bloomfield Road, Moseley	York Road (changed 1902)
Dads Lane (or Dods Lane), Moseley	Dads Lane Road (mentioned 1774)
Doris Road, Small Heath	Atlas Road (changed 1900)
Eachelhurst Road, Pype Hayes	Lodge Road (mentioned 1804)
Edwards Road, Erdington	The Croft (changed 1907)
Ellen Street, Brookfields	Beswick Street (changed 1874)
Emerson Road, Harborne	Highfield Road (changed 1897)
Ethel Street	Post Office Place (changed 1874)

Further Reading

Michael J. Arkinstall and Patrick C. Baird	*Erdington Past and Present* (Birmingham: 1982 edition)
Geoff Bateson	*A History of Castle Vale* (Birmingham: 1998)
A. H. Bevan	'Birmingham Street Names' (City Surveyors Department, unpublished manuscript no date)
Vivian Bird	*Portrait of Birmingham* (London 1970).
Vivian Bird	*Streetwise. Street Names in and about Birmingham* (Oldbury: 1991)
Birmingham Library Services	*The Changing Face of Pype Hayes* (Birmingham: 1994)
H. A. Botwood	*A History of Aston Manor Past and Present* (Birmingham: 1889)
John Thackray Bunce	*History of Old Saint Martin's, Birmingham* (Birmingham: 1875)
John Thackray Bunce	*History of the Corporation of Birmingham with a Sketch of the Early Government of the Town. Vol. I.* (Birmingham: 1878)
Philip B. Chatwin	*A History of Edgbaston* (Birmingham: 1914)
Linda Chew	*Images of Stirchley* (Birmingham: 1995)
Ronald E. Crook	*Kingstanding Past and Present* (Birmingham: 1968)
Kathleen Dayus	*Her People* (London: 1982)
G. Dowling, B.D. Giles and C. Hayfield	*Selly Oak Past and Present* (Birmingham: 1987)
William Dugdale	*Antiquities of Warwickshire* (1656)
Dugdale Society	*The Records of King Edward's School Birmingham. Vol. I. The 'Miscellenay' Volume* (Oxford: 1924)
Jerry Dutton and Colin Green	*Castle Bromwich. – 1066 to 1700* (Castle Bromwich: 1999)

English Life Publications   *Aston Hall* (Derby: no date)

Henry John Everson   *Everson's Moseley, King's Heath and Balsall
                                   Heath Directory and Year Book* (Birmingham:
                                   1896)

Oliver Fairclough   *The Grand Old Mansion. The Holtes and Their
                                   Successors at Aston Hall 1618-1864* (Birmingham:
                                   1984)

Alison Fairn   *A History of Moseley* (Birmingham: 1973)

William Fowler   *A History of Erdington* (Birmingham: 1885)

J. Newton Friend   *Forgotten Aston Manor in Birmingham*
                                   (Birmingham: 1965)

F. W. Hackwood   *Handsworth: Old and New* (Birmingham: 1908).

Joseph Hill and   *Memorials of The Old Square* (Birmingham: 1897)
Robert K. Dent

Michael Hodgetts   Midlands Catholic Buildings (Birmingham: 1990)

George Jacob Holyoake   *Sixty Years of an Agitator's Life* (London: 1906)

F. E. Hopkins   *Cotteridge and its Churches before 1911*
                                   (Birmingham: 1986)

William Hutton   *History of Birmingham to the end of 1780*
                                   (Birmingham: 1780)

John Morris Jones   *The Manor of Handsworth. An Introduction to its
                                   Historical Geography* (Birmingham: 1983 edition)

John Morris Jones   *The Swanshurst Quarter* (Birmingham: no date)

J. A. Langford   'Birmingham Names' in Birmingham and Midland
                                   Institute Archaeological Section *Transactions*
                                   (Birmingham: 1870)

John Alfred Langford   *A Century of Birmingham Life or a Chronicle of
                                   Local Events, from 1741 to 1841. Volumes I and II*
                                   (Birmingham 1868)

John Alfred Langford   *Modern Birmingham and its Institutions. A
                                   chronicle of Local Events from 1841 to 1871
                                   Volumes I and II* (Birmingham: 1873-7)

Francis W. Leonard	*The Story of Selly Oak Birmingham* (Birmingham: 1933)
Arthur B. Lock	*The History of King's Norton and Northfield Wards* (Birmingham: no date)
Joseph McKenna	*Birmingham Street Names* (Birmingham: 1986)
Joseph McKenna	*Birmingham Place Names* (Birmingham: 1988)
Bob Marsden	*ABC of Small Heath and Bordesley Green Past and Present* (Birmingham: 1987)
H.W. Mason	*Austin Village Preservation Society* (Birmingham: no date)
Norman Meacham (put together by Kenneth A. Jones	*A Historical Tour Around Erdington* (Birmingham: 1987)
Rita Morton	*The Building of the Elan Valley Dams* (Birmingham: no date)
Northfield Society	*Recollections of Victorian and Edwardian Northfield* (Birmingham: 1983)
Alma Organ	*Aston During the Nineteenth Century* (unpublished manuscript: no date)
Ian Piper (compiled)	*We Never Slept. The Story of 605 Squadron* (Tamworth: 1996)
Valerie A. Preece	*Duddeston and Vauxhall Gardens* (Birmingham: 1990)
Tom Presterne	*Harborne. 'Once Upon a Time'* (Birmingham: 1913)
Mary and Walter Reynolds	*Memories of King's Heath* (Birmingham: 1989)
Anthony N. Rosser	*The Quinton and Round About. A History. Volume 1* (Birmingham: 1998)
L.F. Salzman (editor)	*The Victoria History of the County of Warwick. Volume IV. Hemlingford Hundred* (London: 1947)
Walter Showell	*Dictionary of Birmingham* (Oldbury: 1885)
Pearson and Rollason	*The Birmingham Directory* (1777)
Victor Skipp	*Medieval Yardley* (London: 1970)

Victor Skipp

A History of Greater Birmingham – down to 1830 (Birmingham: 1980)

Joseph Toulmin Smith

Memorials of Old Birmingham. Men and Names (Birmingham: 1864)

William Hawkes Smith (Printed by James Drake)

The Picture of Birmingham (Birmingham: 1825)

W. B. Stephens (editor)

The Victoria History of the County of Warwick. Volume VII. The City of Birmingham (London: 1964)

Will Thorne

My Life's Battles (London: 1925)

William West

The History, Topography and Directory of Warwickshire (Birmingham: 1830)

Francis White

History, Gazeteer and Directory of Warwickshire (Sheffield: 1850)

Frances Wilmot

The History off Harborne Hall (Birmingham: 1991)

Donald Wright

Bygone Bartley Green (Birmingham: about 1977)

Donald Wright

An Account of Harborne from Earliest Times to 1891 (Birmingham: 1981)

R. Wrightson

Wrightson's New Triennial Directory (Birmingham: 1818)

Maps

John Bartholomew	*Bartholomew's New and Revised Plan of Greater Birmingham* (about 1904)
John Bartholomew	*Bartholomew's Pocket Atlas and Guide to Birmingham* (1954)
Samuel Bradford	*A Plan of Birmingham Surveyed in 1750* (1751)
Bradshaw	*Plan of Birmingham* (1840)
J. W. Brown	*Street Map of the Manor of Aston* (1883)
Ebenezer Robins	*Plan of Birmingham* (1820)
W. Augustus Davies	*Map of the District of Aston Manor (1894)*
James Drake	*Plan of Birmingham* (1832)
James Drake	*Map of Birmingham Divided into Wards* (1835)
W. Fowler	*Aston Manor in 1833* (1835)
J. A. Guest	*Plan of Birmingham 1834 (1837)*
Kelly	*Kelly's Directory Map of Birmingham (1896)*
J. Kempson	*To the Commissioners of the Street Acts, this map of Birmingham shewing the boundaries as perambulated by them in 1810 (1811)*
J. Kempson	*Town of Birmingham* (about 1818)
King's Norton Joint Committee	*Map* (1894)
T. Hanson	*Plan of Birmingham* (1778)
T. Hanson	*Plan of Birmingham* (1781)
Ordnance Survey Office	*Edition of 1914* (scale of 1 to 2,500)
Ordnance Survey Office	*Edition of 1916* (scale of 1 to 2,500)
J. Pigott Smith	*Map of Birmingham engraved from a minute trogonometrical survey made in 1824 and 1825* (1828)
J. Pigott Smith	*Street Map of the Borough of Birmingham* (1855)
C. Pye	*Plan of Birmingham Survey'd in 1795* (1795)
Society for the Diffusion of Useful Knowledge	*Birmingham* (1839)
William S. Till	*Street map of the Borough of Birmingham* (1884)
J. Tomlinson	*Plan of Aston Manor* (1758)

J. Tomlinson	*Plan of Duddeston and Netchells Manors* (1758)
J. Tomlinson	*A Map of Little Bromwich Manor* (1759)
J. Tomlinson	*A Map of Bordesley Manor* (1760)
J. Tomlinson	*A Map of Saltley Manor* (1760)
W. Westley	*The Plan of Birmingham Survey'd in 1731* (1731)

Letters

All letters are in the BirminghamLives Archive, **www.BirminghamLives.co.uk**., developed through South Birmingham College: Jenny Carr 10.9.03; Jack Crockett 29.8.99; Margery Elliott no date; Roger Henney June 2001; Denise Meredith 3.3.2000, Den Rathbone 5.5.97; Matthew Ravenhill 8.9.03; Margaret Read 18.10.97; Ken Roberts 15.12. 2000; Val Robinson 28.8.99; and Norman A. Worwood 13.9.99 I also thank Mrs I. Beeston, M. Clark and Bill Drew for their letters and Jim Hyland for his interest.

INDEX

F.

G.

H.